how2become

Life in the UK Test

www.How2Become.com

D1464782

As part of this product you have also received FREE access to online tests that will help you to pass the Life in the UK Test

To gain access, simply go to:

www.PsychometricTestsOnline.co.uk

Get more products for passing any test at:

www.How2Become.com

Orders: Please contact How2Become Ltd, Suite 14, 50 Churchill Square Business Centre, Kings Hill, Kent ME19 4YU.

You can order through Amazon.co.uk under ISBN 9781911259053, via the website www.How2Become.com or through Gardners.com.

ISBN: 9781911259053

First published in 2016 by How2Become Ltd.

Typeset for How2Become Ltd by Anton Pshinka.

Disclaimer

CONTENTS

INTRODUCTION

Hello, and welcome to your *Life in the UK Test: Revision Guide*. If you are reading this, then the chances are you've decided to become a British citizen. This is a brave and exciting choice which will have fantastic benefits for you. However, it's also time-consuming and expensive. The application process is long and arduous. Luckily, this guide is here to help! This is the first book in our *British Citizen Series*, and will provide you with a complete breakdown of the testing process. You'll be given a comprehensive overview of EVERYTHING you need to learn in order to become a British citizen. The study materials from this book have been taken from the Home Office Publication, *Life in the United Kingdom: A guide for new residents.* It's essential to make sure that you learn as much as you possibly can from these chapters, as the questions that you will be asked during your test are based on the information provided in them. The material from this book will cover everything that is needed in order for you to pass the third edition of the test, which was launched in 2013.

In this book, you'll find information on:

- What the Life in the UK Test involves;
- What type of questions you'll be asked;
- The history of the United Kingdom (UK);
- Important information about the modern UK;
- Essential details on everything from politics to religion;
- And much more!

At the time of writing (September 2016) the price to take the Life in the UK Test is a whopping £50. Every time you re-take, you'll need to pay out beforehand. Thus you won't just be spending your time, but your money too; hopefully this should give you even more incentive to pass the first time!

The aim of this book is to help you SAVE money. By studying this guide, and our companion books, you can make sure that you ace the test on your very first attempt! With our help, and the right commitment, you truly can become a certified British citizen.

How to Use this Guide

To pass the Life in the UK Test, you'll need to revise extremely hard. There are an awful lot of topics that you'll need to revise; from history to politics. To help make the learning process as easy as possible, we've broken this book up into manageable sections. Each of these sections has been specifically designed to enhance your learning. At the end of each section you'll find a handy mock test so that you can recap on what you've learned.

The sections in this guide include:

- The Life in the UK Test: General Info;
- The United Kingdom;
- Britain Through The Ages;
- Modern Day Britain;
- The UK Government;
- UK Law and Order.

Each of these subsections has been broken down into smaller subsections, to give you a detailed insight into British life. You can tackle these sections in any order that you would like, but it's important to make sure that you cover every single one in as much detail as possible.

Applying to Become a Resident of the UK

In order to become a citizen of the United Kingdom, you'll need the following:

- You must be able to speak and read in English;
- You must have a good understanding of living in the UK, and what this requires;
- You must be able to pass the Life in the UK Test.

In order to become a British citizen, you will need to provide good evidence that you have speaking and listening skills in English at B1 of the European Framework of Reference. There are a wide variety of tests that you can take and these tests vary in whether they test speaking and listening skills only, or combine this with reading and writing tests.

In this book, we'll provide you with essential knowledge that will help you prepare for taking the Life in the UK Test.

The Life in the UK Test

The Life in the UK Test is a computer-based assessment. Passing the test is one of the requirements for anyone who is seeking Indefinite Leave to Remain in the United Kingdom, or seeking naturalisation as a British citizen. You won't need to take the test if you are under the age of 18, or over the age of 65. Once you have passed, you won't need to take the test again.

The test will assess you on your knowledge of Britain's past and present. While you won't need to remember dates of birth or death, you will need to have a strong historical understanding of Britain in order to pass.

The Life in the UK Test has 24 multiple-choice questions, and lasts for 45 minutes. The questions are chosen at random, and in order to pass, you need to achieve a mark of at least 75%. So that means, out of 24 questions, you will need to get at least 18 correct. The test is taken in English, although special arrangements can be made for anyone who would prefer to take the test in Welsh or in Scottish Gaelic.

In order to take the Life in the UK Test, you'll need to book your test online at https://www.gov.uk/life-in-the-uk-test. The test can only be taken at a government registered test centre. There are 60 Life in the UK Test centres across the UK. If you take the test at any other establishment, without governmental permission, the results will be not be accepted.

When you book your test, you will need:

- **An email address.** This will be used to contact you/confirm your test date;
- **A debit or credit card.** To take payment for the test;

- **An accepted form of ID.** To ensure that you are a legitimate candidate. Accepted forms of ID include: a passport (which can be out of date), a UK driving licence, an EU identity card, an immigration status document with a UK residence permit, or a biometric residence permit.

When booking your test, it is essential that the name given on your test booking matches exactly with the ID that you use to book the test. You must include your full name, with any middle names, or you will be rejected.

After you've booked your test, you may need to wait for a short while before taking it. You are able to cancel your test without charge for up to 7 days after booking, but after those 7 days, you will not receive a refund in the event of cancellation.

Once you arrive at the test centre, you'll need to be registered, so make sure you get there as early as possible. You'll be required to sign a document confirming your attendance, and will be given the opportunity to take some practice questions prior to taking the actual test. These questions won't count towards your actual mark, and are just there to help you become familiar with the testing software.

If you pass the test, then you will be provided with a Pass Notification Letter. You'll need to sign this before you leave the centre, before taking it with you and sending it off as part of your citizenship application. It is essential that you keep this safe, as you won't be able to get a replacement.

In the event that you fail, you'll be eligible to book and pay for the test again, but you'll need to wait for at least 7 days before doing so.

Why Do I Need to Take the Test?

The Life in the UK Test provides demonstrable proof that you have sufficient knowledge of life and language in the United Kingdom. If you are applying for Indefinite Leave to Remain (also known as settlement) or British citizenship, then passing the test is a necessity. In order to meet the requirements, you'll need to:

- Pass the Life in the UK Test;

- Obtain a speaking and listening qualification in English at B1 CEFR or higher, or its equivalent. If you have a degree-level qualification in English (or higher), then you won't need to take a language test. Likewise, you won't need to take a language test if you are from a country where English is the majority spoken language.

Which Areas Should I Study?

As mentioned, you should try to learn as much as you possibly can from the chapters of this book. From chapter 1 onwards (this chapter not included), all of the material is testable and could appear in your exam. However, you will not need to remember dates of birth or death. Instead, you will be expected to identify when key events happened, or when particular individuals lived. For example, you won't be asked 'What year was Shakespeare born in?' but you might be asked, 'In 1564, which famous playwright was born?' In our end-of-chapter summary revision questions, we've included a couple of date questions, but this is only to help you remember.

In regards to learning dates, there are also a few exceptions. You will need to know the dates for important festivals and events. For example, if you are asked what date Christmas falls on, you will be expected to answer with December 25th. Likewise, with movable festivals such as Easter, you'll need to know the month of the year in which they occur.

When it comes to learning about famous figures, events and even law, you'll need to take a very comprehensive approach. By this we mean that you need to learn everything in the text, not just one or two things. For example, you can't just learn that Charlie Chaplin was an actor. You need to learn that he was an actor in silent movies, who became one of the first British talents to make it into Hollywood. Essentially, don't take the contents of this book as individual/separate facts. You need to learn all of the facts collectively, and be able to explain them in your own way.

Now, let's start by taking a look at the United Kingdom as a whole.

THE UNITED KINGDOM

The United Kingdom (UK) consists of England, Scotland, Wales and Northern Ireland. This is officially known as the 'United Kingdom of Great Britain and Northern Ireland'. Throughout this book, we will use the term 'Britain' to refer to the four aforementioned countries as a whole, but it should be noted that the term 'Great Britain' refers only to England, Scotland and Wales. The rest of Ireland, known as the Republic of Ireland, is an independent country.

The UK owns a number of overseas territories, including locations such as the Falklands Islands and St Helena. While these territories are linked to the UK, they aren't actually a part of it. There are also a number of islands which are closely linked with the UK, but are not a part of it. For example, the Channel Islands and the Isle of Man. These are known as 'Crown dependencies', and have their own governments. The UK is governed by the parliament, which is located in Westminster. Scotland, Wales and Northern Ireland have their own parliaments and assemblies, but these have less power than the UK parliament.

Before we begin looking into the history of Britain, let's briefly examine the UK and how it interacts with the rest of the world.

The Commonwealth

The Commonwealth is an association of countries, which work together for the purposes of democracy and international development. Britain is at the very head of the Commonwealth. The majority of members were once a part of the British Empire. The Queen is the head of the Commonwealth, which currently has 53 states in total. Membership is entirely voluntary, and the members of the Commonwealth are not governed by the group, which holds no power over its members.

The members of the Commonwealth are as follows:

Antigua and Barbuda	Australia	The Bahamas	Bangladesh
Barbados	Belize	Botswana	Brunei Darussalam
Cameroon	Canada	Cyprus	Dominica

Fiji	Ghana	Grenada	Guyana
India	Jamaica	Kenya	Kiribati
Lesotho	Malawi	Malaysia	Maldives
Malta	Mauritius	Mozambique	Namibia
Nauru	New Zealand	Nigeria	Pakistan
Papua New Guinea	Rwanda	Samoa	Seychelles
Sierra Leone	Singapore	Solomon Islands	South Africa
Sri Lanka	St Kitts and Nevis	St Lucia	St Vincent and Grenadines
Swaziland	Tanzania	Tonga	Trinidad and Tobago
Tuvalu	Uganda	UK	Vanuatu
Zambia			

The EU

The European Union (EU) was set up by a group of European Countries, following the signing of the Treaty of Rome in 1957. The EU creates laws for European countries, and these are legally binding for all member states. Britain became a member of the EU in 1973, but citizens voted to leave in a 2016 referendum. It will take approximately two/three years for Britain to fully exit the EU; so it is estimated that the country will leave in 2019. The consequences of this decision are currently unclear, and there is a lot of confusion over how the decision to leave the EU could impact the rights of non-British citizens, as well as British people abroad.

The Council of Europe

Britain is a member of the Council of Europe, which has 46 other member states. It is Europe's leading human rights organisation. The Council is separate from the EU, and cannot make laws, but it draws up both conventions and charters – such as the European Convention on Human Rights.

The United Nations

The UK also belongs to the United Nations, an international organisation which contains 193 member states. The aim of the organisation is to promote international peace and resolve disputes amicably. The UN was set up after the Second World War, and has a 15 member Security Council, of which Britain is a permanent member.

NATO

Finally, the UK is also a member of the North Atlantic Treaty Organisation (NATO). This is a group of European and North American countries, who are allied with each other in the event of an attack. The aim of the group is to maintain peace and respect between its members.

The Values of the United Kingdom

The United Kingdom operates under a set of essential principles, which all people residing within the UK are expected to respect. Being a British citizen is a fantastic privilege. The fundamental values of the UK are based on a long history, and these values are protected and backed up by law. They include:

- **Democracy.**

Britain is a democracy, meaning that those running the country are chosen by the public, and key decisions are made only with public support and backing.

- **Tolerance.**

Britain does not accept extremism or intolerance. Every person in Britain has equal rights and discrimination is illegal.

- **Keeping to the law.**

As a citizen of the United Kingdom, you will be expected to follow and respect the laws of the country.

- **Freedom of speech/belief.**

The UK operates under a system of total freedom of speech and belief – although hate speech is illegal.

- **The right to a fair trial.**

Every single resident of the UK has the right to a fair trial.

Once you have passed the tests to become a British citizen, you'll take part in the citizenship ceremony. This is essentially a big celebration, which provides the opportunity for new citizens to be welcomed into the nation. It is a requirement for you to attend this ceremony if you wish to become a fully naturalised/registered British citizen, and will cost £80 to attend.

During your ceremony, you will need to recite the oath of allegiance, which is as follows:

'I will give my loyalty to the United Kingdom and respect its rights and freedoms. I will uphold its democratic values. I will observe its laws faithfully and fulfil my duties and obligations as a British citizen.'

You must dress formally for the event. You'll be presented with a certificate, photographed in front of a picture of the Queen and be required to sing the National Anthem. The words to this anthem will be contained in your ceremony welcome pack.

Now, let's take a look at the history of the UK.

BRITAIN THROUGH THE AGES

THE STONE AGE

The very first residents of Britain lived in what is known as the Stone Age. These people were hunter-gatherers. The Stone Age was a period in history where people used stone to produce tools and weapons. In date terms, the Stone Age can be divided into three periods:

- **The Old Stone Age (Palaeo*lithic**).** This lasted from the first time that stones were used, until the end of the final Ice Age.

- **The Middle Stone Age *(Meso*lithic**).** This lasted from the end of the final Ice Age, until the introduction of farming.

- **The New Stone Age *(Neo*lithic**).** This lasted from the introduction of farming, until the first time that metal was used.

*The word '*lithic*' refers to stone or rock. It originates from Ancient Greece.

The ancient site of Stonehenge

If you are familiar with the geography of Britain, you'll know that the country is separated from the rest of Europe by the English Channel. However, it hasn't always been that way. For the majority of the Stone Age, Britain was linked to Europe via a land bridge. People used this land bridge to move in and out of the country; hunting deer and other animals. Then, in 6100 BC, a mega-tsunami occurred; striking Britain with enormous force. This turned low-lying ground into what is now known as the North Sea, and southern marshlands into the English Channel. Thus, Britain became an island. There were only around 5,000 residents of the country at the time, and these residents were both scattered and physically frail.

The first farmers in Britain arrived around 6,000 years ago. They had an enormous impact on Britain as we know it today, and built houses and monuments – such as Stonehenge. Prehistoric villages such as Skara Brae are still around today, and have gone a long way to educating us on how our ancestors lived.

The prehistoric village, Skara Brae

THE BRONZE AGE & THE IRON AGE

Following the Stone Age, Britain had the Bronze Age. Like the Stone Age, the Bronze Age was so named as it was the period where people learned how to make bronze. During this age, people lived in roundhouses, and buried their dead in tombs called round barrows. They were highly skilled in crafting objects such as tools and weapons, which were made from materials such as bronze and gold. The result was a myriad of beautiful creations, many of which still exist in museums around Britain.

After the Bronze Age, came the Iron Age. In this period, people learned how to use iron for weapons and tools. They continued to live in roundhouses, but also constructed larger sites called hill forts. A hill fort was essentially a well-defended settlement, which as you might guess, was built on a hill or elevated piece of land. One such example was Maiden Castle in Dorset, which still exists today. During the Iron Age, people spoke in a language/tongue which had Celtic origin. This language was similar to other countries in Europe, and many key assets of this speech are still used in countries such as Scotland and Wales. The majority of people living at this time worked as farmers, crafters or warriors.

Along with all this, the people of the Iron Age also contributed hugely to British history, in that they were the first people to create minted British coins. These coins were inscribed with the names of kings. For this reason, most historians view the Iron Age as the beginning of recorded British history.

THE ROMAN EMPIRE

In 55BC, Julius Caesar – then the general of the Roman army – attempted an invasion of Britain. He failed, and his later attempts to take the country were also unsuccessful. Then, after almost 100 years, the Emperor Claudius led one last attack. Despite the best efforts of leaders such as Boudicca, Britain was conquered. There is a statue of Boudicca on Westminster Bridge, near the Houses of Parliament, which recognises her efforts in keeping the Romans at bay.

Boudicca is commemorated on Westminster Bridge

While the Romans managed to take most of Britain, there were areas of Scotland which remained independent. To keep out the rambunctious rebels, who understandably didn't take well to the Roman invasion, the Emperor Hadrian constructed what is famously known as Hadrian's Wall. Many parts of this wall still remain, such as the forts of Housesteads and Vindolanda; the site is a major British tourist attraction. It is a listed UNESCO (United Nations Educational, Scientific and Cultural Organisation) World Heritage site and is very popular with walkers.

The Romans had an enormous impact on Britain as we know it. They constructed roads and other buildings, created laws which remain to this day and introduced new species and ecosystems to the British countryside. They were here for 400 years, during which time religious Christian communities began to flourish and grow.

Anglo-Saxon Invasion

After 400 years, with the Roman Empire struggling to balance the massive territory it now held, the Romans left Britain to defend other areas of land. They left in AD 410, and never returned. This left Britain open to invasion from other European tribes, such as the Saxons, the Angles and the Jutes. By AD 600, Britain was under Anglo-Saxon rule. This had a huge impact on the language spoken in modern Britain, with many elements of modern language originating from this period of time. As with the Romans, many areas of Scotland resisted and remained free from Anglo-Saxon rule. A similar situation unfolded with people in what is now Wales.

While religion began to prosper in Roman Britain, it was in Anglo-Saxon Britain that it really took shape. While the Anglo-Saxons were not Christians when they first arrived in Britain, over time missionaries from across Europe arrived, preaching about Christianity. Famous Christian Irish missionaries such as St Patrick and St Columba made their names by spreading the word of God across the country. St Augustine led missionaries from Rome, who spread Christianity in the south. St Augustine was later named the first Archbishop of Canterbury, a role which remains hugely significant today.

VIKINGS

In 789 AD, the Vikings arrived. Warriors from Norway and Denmark, they initially raided coastal towns, taking away expensive goods and even slaves. After the Anglo-Saxon kingdoms in Britain united under King Alfred the Great, the Vikings were defeated. The result of this was that many of the invaders remained in the country, in an area known as the Danelaw, and settled/mixed with local communities. Areas such as Grimsby are named based on Viking languages. The Viking invasion had a significant impact on Scotland too. The threat of attack and the efficiency of the unified Anglo-Saxon army persuaded the people of the north to unite under one king – Kenneth MacAlpin. This marked the beginning of when the term 'Scotland' started to be used.

THE NORMANS

In 1066, one of the most famous battles in British history took place. William, Duke of Normandy, led his forces against Harold Godwinson, the Saxon King of England. This became known as the Battle of Hastings. After several hours, and many casualties, it became clear that William was losing. The Norman Forces could not break through the English shield wall. Harold had superior position and numbers on his side. However, he was outsmarted by William, who feigned retreat, before turning around and slaughtering the English forces. Harold was defeated, supposedly killed by a stray arrow (although this has been questioned by many historians). William had won.

William marched through the South, and on Christmas Day 1066 he was crowned King of England. The events of the battle were commemorated in a famous piece of embroidery, known as the Bayeux Tapestry. This can still be viewed in France. Following his takeover, William became known as William the Conqueror.

The Norman Conquest had massive consequences for British history. Modern day English has strong roots in Norman French, the language imposed by the new ruling class. Once again, Scotland and Wales opposed the new rulers. Wales was initially conquered, but gradually took more and more land back, whereas Scotland could not be invaded.

One of the most important events during William's reign was the creation of the Domesday Book. The Domesday Book listed all of the towns and villages in England, along with the people who lived in there, what land they owned and what animals they owned. It is the oldest surviving public record, and has been invaluable for historians in studying British history.

Now test out what you've learned with our revision quiz. You'll find full mock tests at the back of the book!

Revision Quiz

Q1. What was the Stone Age named after?

Q2. What created the English Channel?

Q3. What is a hill fort?

Q4. Where did people live during the Bronze Age?

Q5. Why was Hadrian's Wall constructed?

Q6. Name two famous British missionaries.

Q7. Who fought in the battle of Hastings, and who was the victor?

Q8. What was in the Domesday Book?

See the next page for the answers!

Answers

1. The Stone Age was named after the development of stone tools and weapons during this time.

2. The English Channel was created by a mega-tsunami, which turned southern marshlands into the English Channel.

3. A hill fort was a well-defended settlement built on a hill or elevated piece of land.

4. During the Bronze Age, people lived in roundhouses.

5. Hadrian's Wall was constructed to keep out Scottish rebels, who didn't accept the Roman invasion of Britain.

6. St Patrick and St Columba.

7. Harold Godwinson fought against William, Duke of Normandy. William was the victor.

8. The Domesday Book listed all of the towns and villages in England, along with the people who lived in there, what land they owned and what animals they owned.

THE MIDDLE AGES

Following the Norman Conquest, Britain went through a period known as the Middle Ages. This period lasted until 1485, and was marked by a number of wars. Namely, amongst the English, Welsh, Scottish and Irish.

In 1284, the Statute of Rhuddlan was introduced, which attempted to establish English rule in Wales. Despite numerous Welsh rebellions, by the 15th century England had taken complete control of Wales, and English laws and language were imposed. England also established rule over certain areas of Ireland, such as the Pale, in Dublin. Meanwhile, the Scottish remained unconquerable. Led by Robert Bruce, they dealt defeat to the English at the Battle of Bannockburn in 1314.

The wars weren't just confined to what we now know as the United Kingdom either. Wars abroad were common. Some of the most famous of these include the Crusades – where European Christians battled for ownership of the Holy Land, and the Hundred Years War – between Britain and France. The Hundred Years War resulted in famous battles such as the Battle of Agincourt in 1415, where the English defeated the French. The English later left France, in the 1450s.

Battle of Agincourt in 1415. Engraved by J.Rogers

The Middle Ages saw the development of Britain into an essential trading nation. English wool was an extremely valuable commodity; Britain itself became a popular place for foreigners to trade and work as a result. This brought skilled labourers over too, resulting in significant architectural improvements. Castles started to be built in England and Ireland, for defence. Also, great cathedrals – such as Lincoln Cathedral – were built. Many of these buildings are still used for worship, and used stained glass windows to tell stories about the Bible.

Law and Parliament

Today's system of government has strong roots in the Middle Ages. During this period, Parliament began to develop. It started out as a small council of advisors, noblemen and church leaders, and steadily grew into something much larger.

These noblemen instigated a significant power shift. Up until 1215, the power of the king had been almost unlimited. While there existed a 'King's Council' who would offer advice, their views did not necessarily have to be taken into account. This all changed once King John took the throne. Appalled by his cruelty, the nobles forced John to agree to a charter of rights called the Magna Carta. This was groundbreaking, and established a principle that the King was subject to law, and could not just act of his own accord. In order to make big decisions, such as changing taxes or laws; the king would need to consult with the noblemen first. This would be known as Parliament.

The Magna Carta being signed by King John, 1215, illustration by John Leech

Gradually, the number of people attending Parliament grew, and two houses were established:

- **The House of Lords.**

This house consisted of the nobility in society. For example, landowners and bishops.

- **The House of Commons.**

This house consisted of smaller landowners, knights and wealthy people from towns/cities.

The Middle Ages brought about significant changes for judges; in that judges began to be chosen by merit, or precedence; where previously they had simply been an extension of the government.

The Normans also brought feudalism to England. Feudalism was a system which managed the relationship between the king, landowners and peasants. The king provided lords with land; in exchange for them providing men/ soldiers during war. Peasants were given a small area of their lord's land, where they were entitled to grow food; but they had to work for their lord in exchange and were not allowed to move away. There were serious flaws in this system, which later came to a head during the Peasants' Revolt of 1381.

Language and Writing

The Middle Ages were a really important time for language development and literature. As mentioned, William was of Norman descent. This meant that the common tongue of the king and his noblemen was Norman-French, but this was in contrast to the Anglo-Saxon English spoken by the lower class. After a while, the two languages merged, to form one English language. The language spoken in Britain today contains words from both Norman-French and Anglo-Saxon vocabulary. By 1400, the language was nationally spoken and was being used in royal court and Parliament. In Scotland, Gaelic remained the dominant language, but the Scottish language began to develop. Prominent poets began writing in Scottish, and slowly its influence grew.

In line with this, the Middle Ages saw the creation of one of the most famous literary works of all time. *The Canterbury Tales* by Geoffrey Chaucer tells the story of a pilgrimage to Canterbury. It is a collection of poems, from the fictional characters on the pilgrimage. The book was printed by William Caxton, who was the very first person in England to print using a printing press. The stories told in *The Canterbury Tales* remain extremely popular to this day, and many have been adapted for TV and theatre.

Disease

The Middle Ages also marked the introduction of the Black Death to Britain. This was a form of plague, which resulted in fatal symptoms. After spreading across other areas of Europe, the disease arrived here in 1348. The results were catastrophic, and England, Scotland and Wales all lost approximately one third of their populations. Britain (and the rest of Europe) continued to be hit by fresh waves of the disease all the way up until the late 1600s, resulting in millions of deaths. It is regarded as one of the worst disasters in British history.

The Wars of the Roses

The Wars of the Roses were an infamous series of wars for control of the throne. They were fought between two opposing families: the House of York and the House of Lancaster. The war was named after the sigils of the families, with Lancaster having a red rose and York having a white rose. Many people see the war as being split (loosely) into two parts:

- **Part 1.** Edward IV of House York defeats House Lancaster and takes the throne.

- **Part 2.** Edward dies, Richard of House York takes the throne and is then defeated by Henry Tudor, from House Lancaster. This marked the beginning of the Tudor Dynasty.

The war officially ended at the Battle of Bosworth Field, in 1485. Richard was slain during the battle and Henry took the throne, becoming Henry VII. He married Richard's niece, Elizabeth of York, uniting the two families as one. Henry became the first king of the House of Tudor. To symbolise this alliance, both of the sigils were merged together to form a red rose with a white rose inside of it.

Now test out what you've learned with our revision quiz. You'll find full mock tests at the back of the book!

Revision Quiz

Q1. In 1282, the Statute of Rhuddlan was introduced. What was the purpose of this?

Q2. Who led the Scottish forces at the Battle of Bannockburn, in 1314?

Q3. Which key principle did the Magna Carter establish?

Q4. The two houses of Parliament are the House of Lords and The House of Commons. During the Middle Ages, which type of people presided in the House of Commons?

Q5. What is feudalism (in a general sense) and which event did this culminate in?

Q6. Who wrote *The Canterbury Tales*?

Q7. Why was William Caxton so famous?

Q8. Which battle marked the end of the War of the Roses?

See the next page for the answers!

Answers

1. Attempted to establish English rule in Wales.

2. Robert Bruce.

3. That the King couldn't pass certain laws without agreement from Parliament first.

4. The House of Commons consisted of smaller landowners, knights and wealthy people from towns/cities.

5. Feudalism was a system which managed the relationship between the king, landowners and peasants. This culminated in the Peasants Revolt of 1381.

6. Geoffrey Chaucer.

7. William Caxton was the very first person in England to print using a printing press.

8. Battle of Bosworth Field.

THE TUDORS

Henry VII did his utmost to ensure that there would be no repetition of the Wars of the Roses. In order to ensure this, he took steps to reduce the power of noblemen in England, and put more weight/authority behind the crown. After he died, this was a policy that his son – Henry VIII – continued with.

Henry VIII

Henry VIII is one of the most famous kings in history, and for good reason. His break from the Church of Rome and his six wives have guaranteed that his memory lived on. Henry's behaviour as king has been studied in great detail by historians and psychologists alike, and by many people he is remembered as the archetypal 'tyrant' king.

You are almost certain to be asked at least one question based on Henry VIII, so pay close attention to this section.

Henry's Wives

Henry had six wives over the course of his monarchy. Below we've broken down these marriages in brief detail, to give you an overview of the facts:

Catherine of Aragon. Henry's first wife was Catherine of Aragon. Spanish born, she had a number of children with Henry, but only one child survived. This was a girl named Mary. Disappointed with the lack of male heir, Henry divorced Catherine once she became too old to have children.

Anne Boleyn. Next came Anne Boleyn. English born, Anne gave Henry another daughter, Elizabeth, but miscarried after falling pregnant again. She slowly fell out of favour with Henry's inner circle, and then Henry himself. She was arrested on (probably false) charges of adultery and incest, and was executed at the Tower of London.

Jane Seymour. Jane Seymour was Henry's third wife. She provided Henry with a son, Edward, but died after giving birth.

Anne of Cleves. Henry's fourth wife was Anne of Cleves, a German princess.

Henry married her purely for political reasons but quickly divorced her after realising that he didn't find her attractive. Following the divorce, Henry and Anne became great friends.

Catherine Howard. Catherine Howard was a cousin of Anne Boleyn, and was very young when she married Henry. Their marriage did not last long. Like Anne Boleyn, Catherine was accused of adultery and executed.

Catherine Parr. Catherine Parr was Henry's final wife. She outlived Henry, before marrying again, but died shortly after.

Henry and Religion

Along with his marriages, Henry is also famous for the sweeping changes that he brought to religion. In order to divorce Catherine of Aragon (his first wife) Henry needed to gain the permission of the Pope. Unfortunately the Pope refused. Enraged by this decision, Henry took matters into his own hands. He set up his own church. This was known as the Church of England. In this church, the king had the power to decide how worship should be done, grant divorces and appoint bishops.

While Henry's decision might seem rash, it was actually part of a wider movement of the times. People across Europe were becoming disillusioned with the authority of the Pope and were striking out against the Roman Catholic Church. Groups such as Protestants set up their own churches, refused to read in Latin and stopped believing in the authority of the church as a vessel for God. They did not pray to saints or shrines, and believed that a person's own relationship with God was more important than submitting to the Church.

Henry followed this up by closing down Roman Catholic Abbeys, Monasteries and convents across England, Ireland and Wales. However, despite all this, England remained a Catholic country until Henry's death in 1547.

Henry also passed the Act for the Government of Wales. This united the two countries, with Welsh representatives in Parliament and a reformation of the Welsh legal system. Despite this, attempts to enforce the same values in Ireland did not go down so well, and led to open rebellion from Irish leaders.

Once Henry died, his son Edward took the throne. Edward was a devout Protestant, who introduced the Book of Common Prayer to the Church of England. Under Edward's rule, England became a Protestant country and Catholics were treated very badly. However, Edward died at the age of 15, after which his half-sister Mary became queen. In huge contrast to Edward, Mary was a Catholic. She became known as 'Bloody Mary' after her harsh treatment towards Protestants, 280 of whom were burned at the stake. After a short reign, Mary died. She was replaced by her half-sister Elizabeth, the daughter of Henry and Anne Boleyn.

Queen Elizabeth I

Queen Elizabeth I is one of the most famous and popular monarchs in British history. Under Elizabeth, Britain found a better religious balance between Catholicism and Protestantism. While it was law to attend your local church, Elizabeth's reign was marked by a lack of religious conflict, which had been so prevalent in the previous reigns. Despite this, Elizabeth was still a Protestant queen, so Catholics fared worse. She introduced the Elizabethan Religious Settlement, which required any public or church office members to swear allegiance to the queen as the head of church and state. Anyone who refused risked imprisonment or even execution. Catholics were largely marginalised by all of this, and resentment festered over into the reign of King James.

In 1588, the Spanish sent an Armada (a large group of ships) to invade England and restore Catholicism as the dominant religion. They were resoundingly beaten by Sir Francis Drake and Charles Howard, the commanders of the British fleet. This added to Elizabeth's huge popularity.

Under Elizabeth, Britain expanded its geographic exploration. This led to the development of new trade routes, and British trading with new colonies. Sir Francis Drake led many of these expeditions. His ship, the *Golden Hind*, was one of the first to sail all the way round the world. During this period, English settlers began to colonise the eastern coast of America. This is something which was greatly expanded upon in the next century.

Elizabeth neither married nor had any children, and so the Tudor dynasty died with her in 1603. However, the impact she and her father left are still felt in Britain today.

Elizabeth's reign is also famous for literary improvements. Chiefly amongst these, the works of a certain playwright...

William Shakespeare

Born in Stratford-upon-Avon, England, William Shakespeare is widely regarded as the finest playwright of all time. His plays and poems are studied and performed frequently today, and his works have had an enormous impact on literature. Many of the most popular works in theatrical and literary history have roots in Shakespearean narratives, themes and concepts. Even the language we speak today has been heavily influenced by Shakespeare, as he invented a number of commonly used words and phrases.

Some of Shakespeare's most popular plays include:

- *Romeo and Juliet*
- *King Lear*
- *Macbeth*
- *A Midsummer Night's Dream*
- *The Taming of the Shrew*

Shakespeare's plays were performed in the Globe Theatre. Today, there exists a modern copy of the Globe Theatre (in London) in which re-enactments are performed.

Mary Queen of Scots

Scotland had been heavily impacted by Protestant reforms. The Protestant Scottish Parliament made Catholicism illegal, and renounced the authority of the Pope. This was unfortunate for the young queen of Scotland, Mary Stuart, who was a Catholic. Mary was just 1 week old when her father died, and she was made queen. She spent the majority of her childhood in France, and returned to a very different Scotland. Forced to flee to England, Mary put her Protestant son, James VI, on the throne. She then sought protection from her cousin, Queen Elizabeth. Elizabeth, however, suspected Mary of trying to take the English throne. This was bolstered by the fact that many Catholics in the country considered Mary to be the rightful heir to the throne. After spending 20 years as a prisoner, Mary was eventually executed for plotting to kill Elizabeth.

Now test out what you've learned, with our revision quiz. You'll find full mock tests at the back of the book!

Revision Quiz

Q1. Henry VIII had six wives. His fifth wife was executed. What was her (full) name?

Q2. Henry's fourth wife was Anne of Cleves. What was the outcome of this marriage, and for what reason?

Q3. What was the purpose of the Elizabethan Religious Settlement?

Q4. In 1588, the Spanish Armada were defeated by the English. Name one of the commanders of the English fleet.

Q5. What was the birthplace of William Shakespeare?

Q6. Name three popular Shakespeare plays.

Q7. What relation was Mary Queen of Scots to Elizabeth I?

Q8. How many children did Queen Elizabeth I have?

See the next page for the answers!

Answers

1. Henry's fifth wife was Catherine Howard.

2. This marriage ended in divorce, as Henry was not attracted to Anne.

3. The Elizabethan Religious Settlement required any public or church office members to swear allegiance to the queen as the head of church and state.

4. Sir Francis Drake.

5. Stratford-upon-Avon.

6. Romeo and Juliet, King Lear, Macbeth *(any that are mentioned in the chapter)*.

7. Cousin.

8. 0.

THE STUARTS

King James

Elizabeth did not marry, and thus produced no children whom could take the throne. When she died in 1603, the immediate heir was Mary's son – James VI of Scotland. James was named King James I of England, Wales and Ireland. Despite this, Scotland remained an entirely independent/separate nation.

James is perhaps most famous for providing a new translation of the Bible, into English. This is known as the King James Version, and is widely used in Protestant churches to this day. James took a far more lenient approach to Catholicism than Elizabeth; he actually reprieved a group of Catholic plotters early in his reign – not wanting to begin with bloodshed. Unfortunately, conflicts with the Pope eventually led to James denouncing the Catholic religion altogether, and Catholic Priests were ordered to leave the country. This meant that his reign was marked by religious turmoil, culminating in The Gunpowder Plot, where a group of disillusioned Catholics plotted to blow up the Houses of Parliament.

James also faced religious rebellions in Ireland, who rejected the Protestant government in England. As a measure of control, the government encouraged Scottish and English Protestants to form 'plantations' in the northern province of Ulster, Ireland. These settlers took the land from Catholic landowners, and this was then repeated in other areas of the country. The settlements that they formed were known as plantations.

Throughout his reign, James had a number of clashes with parliament. He believed in the 'Divine Right of Kings', which was essentially that the king had been chosen by God to rule. This attitude led him to believe that he didn't need Parliament's help to rule the country. Unfortunately, this was an attitude that he passed down to his son – with disastrous consequences.

King James I

Charles I

When James died, his son Charles inherited the throne. Charles immediately took the 'Divine Right of Kings' as a means of ruling. Upon discovering that Parliament would not agree to his policies, he attempted to rule without their approval. He dissolved Parliament in 1629. Unfortunately, Charles ran into severe problems in Scotland. After the introduction of a new/revised Prayer Book was rejected by the Presbyterian Scottish Church, a Scottish army was raised. Unable to raise money for his own army, Charles was forced to recall Parliament to ask it for funds. Unsurprisingly, they outright refused, on the grounds that they disagreed with Charles's religious reforms and views. After another rebellion in Ireland, Parliament demanded control of the English army. Furious, Charles entered the House of Commons and attempted to arrest five parliamentary leaders. The result of this was that in 1642, civil war broke out. On one side were the supporters of the king, known as Cavaliers, and on the other were those who supported Parliament, known as Roundheads.

The civil war led to a number of battles, but by 1646 the Roundheads had established a dominant victory, led by Oliver Cromwell. Defeat in battles such as Marston Moor and Naseby left the king's army crippled; eventually he was taken prisoner. Stubborn to the last, Charles refused to negotiate with Parliament. In 1649 he was executed.

The English Commonwealth

For the first time in hundreds of years, England no longer had a monarch. The nation declared itself a republic, which was known as the Commonwealth. Amid uncertainty about how the country would be ruled, Cromwell travelled to Ireland; where he brutally established the authority of Parliament, resulting in the deaths of thousands of innocent people. To this day, Cromwell is negatively thought of in Ireland. Cromwell also smashed Scottish hopes of placing Charles's son, Charles II, on the throne. Scotland had not agreed to the execution of the king, and sent an army into England with the intent of restoring the monarchy. After defeat at Dunbar and Worcester, Charles fled to the Netherlands. Cromwell was named Lord Protector, and ruled the country until his death in 1658. Following Cromwell's death, his son Richard was announced Lord Protector. This did not work, as Richard lacked his father's ability to control both the army and government. He was not a real leader, and abdicated in May 1659.

Re-Establishing the Monarchy

In 1660, recognising the need for an established leader, parliament made contact with Charles II. He was invited to return from exile, and crowned King Charles II of England, Wales, Scotland and Ireland. Unlike his father, Charles II was far more willing to negotiate with Parliament and accepted that he would need their support and agreement to make decisions. The result was that Charles II and parliament had a far more amicable relationship. He re-established the Church of England as the official church, and initiated the Habeas Corpus Act of 1679. This essentially meant that no person could be held unlawfully as a prisoner, and that every prisoner had the right to a court hearing. This piece of legislation is still in use today.

Introducing Science

Charles II's reign also saw the beginnings of scientific understanding. Charles II was a keen scientist, and sought to increase public awareness of the world around us. Amongst others, the Royal Navy Society (which still exists to this day) was formed, to promote scientific/natural knowledge. A key member of this society was Isaac Newton, who discovered gravity. Newton first became interested in science when he studied at Cambridge University. He went on to publish famous works such as *Mathematical Principles of Natural Philosophy*. Newton also discovered that white light is made up of the colours of the rainbow. These discoveries meant that Newton has had an enormous impact upon modern science.

Rebuilding London

In the early 1660s, news reached England that the plague was once again spreading around Europe. Preventative measures were quickly enforced, with strict monitoring of docks and shipping ports. As reports of more and more European deaths began to spread, England tightened regulations; but it wasn't enough. In 1665, the plague arrived once more and devastated London. Over 100,000 people died from the disease in 1665-1666. This was known as The Great Plague. It was the very last major epidemic of the plague to hit London, and was far lesser in scale than the previous Black Death.

In September 1666, the Great Fire of London devastated the city. Starting in a bakery on Pudding Lane, the blaze spread outwards, carried by a strong gale and the close proximity of the largely wooden buildings. Soon, almost the whole of central London was on fire. The fire lasted from Sunday until Wednesday. Remarkably only 6 deaths have been officially recorded, although this figure has been recently questioned. The social and economic problems resulting from the blaze were enormous. Buildings such as the original St Paul's Cathedral were destroyed. The fire tore through the worst of the plague devastated areas: where rats and fleas had prospered, and in the aftermath London was largely rebuilt as a spacious and open city – to reduce the risk of such disasters occurring in future.

Events such as these were detailed in the famous diary of Samuel Pepys, which was later published and can still be read to this day.

King James II

Charles II had no legitimate heirs; meaning that when he died in 1685, his brother James took the throne. James II was a strong Roman Catholic, with an obvious bias towards members of the Catholic faith. This was to the horror of Parliament, who frequently clashed with him. Just as his father Charles I had done, James did not try to reach agreements with Parliament and even arrested many bishops from the Church of England. As a Protestant country, this alarmed many people, who believed that James was trying to make England fully Catholic once again. James had 3 children – two elder daughters and a young son. His two daughters were Protestant. This was to be his downfall.

The Revolution of 1688

James's daughter Mary was married to William of Orange, the ruler of the Netherlands. William was fiercely Protestant. In 1688, backed by members of Parliament and supporting groups in England; William's army sailed into England. They met no resistance from James, who fled, and William was swiftly pronounced king. This event has been nicknamed the 'Glorious Revolution', because of the fact that there was so little bloodshed in William's campaign, and that it put an end to the idea of a monarch ruling without the need for Parliament. James attempted to regain the throne, but failed. He was defeated at the Battle of Boyne in Ireland (1690), and Scottish rebellions in support of James were largely crushed.

Scottish clans were thereby required to take an oath, swearing fealty to William III, (William II in Scotland). Failure to take the oath had brutal consequences. For example, the MacDonald clan of Glencoe were slaughtered for being late to swear fealty, thus making many Scottish people both fearful and distrustful of the new government. This killing is known as the Glencoe Massacre, and the names of those who died are commemorated on the Glencoe Massacre Memorial Monument, which can be found in Scotland. Based on this, James II continued to garner support in Scotland. His supporters became known as Jacobites, and continued this cause long after James II's death.

Constitutional Bills

During the reign of William and Mary, a number of important constitutional bills were passed. The first of these, passed during their coronation, was the Declaration of Rights. This made it official constitution that the monarch would not be able to raise taxes or deliver justice without agreement from parliament. The Declaration of Rights listed all of the wrongs committed by James II, and 13 clauses which limited royal power, all as a consequence of James's behaviour. Once William and Mary had signed this Declaration, in exchange for their appointment as King and Queen, parliament became the central governing body of law and justice in England. This was followed up by the Bill of Rights in 1689, which gave parliament the power to decide who could be monarch. This monarch had to be a Protestant, and a new parliament would be elected every 3 years (now five years).

All of this was crucial, because it led to the start of party politics as we know them today. In order to push through decisions, the king or queen needed to have advisers who could seal a majority of votes in the two Houses of Parliament: the House of Lords and the House of Commons. Similarly to today, there were two main groups in parliament – the Tories (today the Conservative Party) and the Whigs (comparable to today's Liberal Democrats).

All of these changes marked the beginning of what is commonly known as constitutional monarchy. Constitutional monarchy is the system where whilst the monarch is very important, they cannot pass particular actions or laws if parliament don't agree. Despite this, it wasn't all revolutionary. Members of parliament were voted in by the public, but there was still a serious imbalance in the number of people who could actually vote. Women weren't allowed to vote at all, and only men with certain levels of wealth could vote. In some places, constituencies were completely controlled by just one rich family. These areas became known as 'pocket boroughs'. In other less well-off places, there were barely any voters at all. These areas were known as 'rotten boroughs'.

Population Increase

Throughout this period, Britain's population began to really grow. While people were still leaving the country to settle in places such as America, many more were coming and staying. Protestant refugees from France fled to England after being treated as criminals in their own country. These people were known as Huguenots. Britain also attracted Jews for the first time since the Middle Ages, who settled in London.

Along with the increase in population, Britain also made important developments in free press. From the year 1695 onwards, newspapers could legally operate without the need for a government licence. Until this point, newspapers had largely been controlled by those in charge. Now many more new newspapers sprang up, unburdened from the control of the government.

William and Mary's successor was Queen Anne. Despite numerous pregnancies, Anne died without any surviving children. This created a huge deal of uncertainty, and tensions arose between England, Wales, Ireland and Scotland. Thus, in 1707, the Act of Union was created. This was an act that created the Kingdom of Great Britain, and linked England and Scotland together. It meant that Scotland was no longer an independent country but at the same time could maintain its own legal, educational and religious systems.

Now test out what you've learned, with our revision quiz! You'll find full mock tests at the back of this book!

Revision Quiz

Q1. Despite James's leniency towards Catholics, he eventually alienated them. What was the end result of this?

Q2. Why did James VI clash with parliament?

Q3. Charles I went to war with parliament. The supporters of parliament were known as Roundheads. What was the name for the supporters of the King?

Q4. Who won the war between Charles and parliament, and what was the end result for the monarchy?

Q5. Why is Oliver Cromwell negatively thought of in Ireland?

Q6. What was the Habeas Corpus Act of 1679?

Q7. Who started the Glorious Revolution?

Q8. In 1707, the Act of Union was created. What was this?

See the next page for the answers!

Answers

1. The end result of this was the Gunpowder Plot, where a group of Catholics attempted to blow up the Houses of Parliament.

2. James VI clashed with parliament, as he believed in 'The Divine Right of Kings', meaning he felt he could rule without parliament's help.

3. The name for the supporters of the King was the Cavaliers. ('Royalists' is also acceptable).

4. Parliament won decisively, and Charles was executed. Oliver Cromwell became Lord Protector.

5. Cromwell brutally established the authority of the English Parliament in Ireland, resulting in the deaths of thousands of innocent people.

6. The Glorious Revolution was started by William of Orange, the ruler of the Netherlands.

7. The Habeas Corpus Act established the idea that that no person could be held unlawfully as a prisoner, and that every prisoner had the right to a court hearing.

8. The Act of Union created the Kingdom of Great Britain. It meant that Scotland was no longer an independent country, but at the same time could maintain its own legal, educational and religious systems.

THE GEORGIAN ERA

As per their right to do so, parliament chose the next king. They named George I, who was Anne's nearest relative. George was of German descent, born in Hanover, and therefore spoke fairly poor English. In response to this appointment, an attempt was made by Scottish Jacobites to depose George and place James II's son on the throne. This was swiftly defeated. Due to the language barrier, George relied heavily on his ministers during his reign, and this led to the creation of a hugely significant position – the Prime Minister. This was the name for the most important minister in the Houses of Parliament, and today England is governed by this individual. Sir Robert Walpole was named the very first Prime Minister in 1721. Towards the end of George's reign, Sir Robert was largely in control of ruling the country. George was succeeded by his son, George II.

Bonnie Prince Charlie

In 1745, the Jacobites tried again to depose the ruler (George II) and place a Stuart king on the throne. This time, the rebellion was led by Charles Edward Stuart (nicknamed Bonnie Prince Charlie) – the grandson of James II. With the backing of Scottish clansmen, Charles raised an army, but was defeated at the Battle of Culloden in 1746. He fled to Europe and the rebellion was crushed. Following this loss, measures were taken to prevent such an uprising from happening again. Measures were enforced where chieftains could only become landlords if they had the favour of the English monarch. Clansmen effectively became tenants, who had to pay for the land they inhabited. This gave rise to the Highland Clearances, where Scottish landlords demolished small farms, in order to make space for larger flocks of livestock. The Scottish population also decreased during this period, as large numbers of people left to settle in America.

A monument to Bonnie Prince Charlie

However, it wasn't all bad for Scotland – this period also saw the rise of the prominent Scottish poet, Robert Burns. Known as 'The Bard', Burns produced a number of famous works, the most well-known of which is *Auld Lang Syne.* This is the song that people in the UK (and other countries) sing whilst celebrating New Year.

The Enlightenment

During the 18th century, new ideas about politics, philosophy and science were developed. This is often called 'the Enlightenment'. Many of the great thinkers of the Enlightenment were Scottish. Adam Smith developed ideas about economics which are still referred to today. David Hume's ideas about human nature continue to influence philosophers. Scientific discoveries, such as James Watt's work on steam power, helped the progress of the Industrial Revolution. One of the most important principles of the Enlightenment was that everyone should have the right to their own political and religious beliefs, and that the state should not try to dictate to them. This continues to be an important principle in the UK today.

The Industrial Revolution

The 18th and 19th centuries saw the boom of industry in Britain. Britain was the very first country to industrialise on such an enormous scale, which became known as the Industrial Revolution. Until this period, agriculture had been by far the biggest area of employment in Britain. Goods such as wool and cloth were in high demand. Now, however, factory employment surpassed this. The development of machinery and steam power meant that agriculture and manufacturing could be done via machines; making the process more efficient and the production levels far higher. The need for raw materials such as coal also increased, as these were essential for keeping factories going. As a result of this, many people left the countryside in order to start working in factories or in mining industries. The development of the Bessemer process, for the mass production of steel, caused the shipbuilding and railway industries to boom.

One important figure during this period was Richard Arkwright. Born in 1732, Arkwright initially worked as a barber, dying hair and making wigs, before he went on to make significant improvements to the carding machine. Carding is the process of preparing fibres for spinning into yarn and fabric. He also developed horse driven spinning mills that used only one machine. This increased the efficiency of production. Arkwright is remembered for the efficient and profitable way that he ran his factories.

Unfortunately, there was also a bad side to the Industrial Revolution: namely for the workers. Conditions were appalling. With no laws in place to protect employees, employers could subject their staff to whatever conditions they felt like. Abject wages, dangerous working environments and long hours were all part and parcel of working in a factory. Children were employed and treated in the same way as adults, with fines and beatings a regular occurrence. It was common to pick up chest and lung infections from factories, where dust hung in the warm, damp air; the noise from the machines could also damage hearing. While Unions were established to fight these conditions, the number of people moving to Britain – many of whom were prepared to work under such circumstances – severely weakened the impact of these Unions.

Trading, Slavery and Conflict

During this period, British trading reached new heights. More and more goods began to be imported in and out of the country, such as spices from the West Indies and tea from India. Britain established colonies in Australia, took control of Canada and began to colonise Africa.

All of the above brought Britain into direct conflict with countries such as France, who were doing similar things. In 1789, a revolution occurred in France, and government declared war on Britain. This led to a series of important battles, amongst them:

- **The Battle of Trafalgar.**

The Battle of Trafalgar was fought by Britain's navy, against combined Spanish and French fleets. Britain won the battle, but Admiral Nelson died in combat aboard the *HMS Victory*. Nelson's Column in Trafalgar Square, London, is a tribute to him.

- **The Battle of Waterloo.**

The conflict between France and Britain ended at the Battle of Waterloo, where British forces, commanded by the Duke of Wellington (also known as the Iron Duke), defeated the French force led by Emperor Napoleon. Wellington was later named British Prime Minister.

By the 18th century, the overseas slave trade was absolutely booming. Britain was (unfortunately) at the forefront of this industry. While slavery was illegal in Britain itself, slaves would travel from West Africa – via British ships – to areas such as America and the Caribbean. Once they arrived, they were forced to work on plantations in terrible conditions. Any slaves who tried to escape or revolt were punished severely, sometimes with death. Despite the economic benefits that it brought, many people in Britain were rightly opposed to the slave trade. Anti-slavery groups were set up by religious groups, with the famous William Wilberforce amongst them, and petitions were made to parliament. By 1807, it became illegal for British ships to trade slaves or for slaves to be traded via British ports. In 1833, the Emancipation Act completely abolished slavery of any kind in the British Empire. The Navy was instructed to free slaves from slave ships that they encountered, and punish slave traders. 2 million Indian and Chinese workers were employed to replace the freed slaves in areas such as sugar plantations, mines and railways.

Despite the negative impact of slavery, British foreign relations were leading to important discoveries. Two of these were made by Sake Dean Mahomet. Born in the Bengal region of India, in 1759, Mahomet first arrived in England in 1782. In 1810 he opened the Hindoostane Coffee House in George Street. This was the very first curry house to open in Britain. Along with this, Mahomet and his wife also introduced 'shampooing', the Indian art of head massage, to Britain.

The War of Independence

Britain had established a number of colonies in North America. The colonies were self-governed, had substantial wealth and a good standard of education; the British government wanted to tax them. Unsurprisingly, the colonies were not happy with this, and believed it constituted an attack on their rights and freedom. This was especially the case since they had no representation in parliament. While the government tried to reach a compromise, tensions developed and things rapidly accelerated – leading to the events of 1776, where 13 of the colonies declared independence from the British Empire. War was announced. Spain and France joined the colonies in fighting against Britain, meaning that the British were defeated and forced to recognise the colonies' independence in 1783.

The Union Flag

Although Ireland had the same monarch as England and Wales since Henry VIII, it had remained a separate country. In 1801, Ireland became unified with England, Scotland and Wales after the Act of Union of 1800. This created the United Kingdom of Great Britain and Ireland. One symbol of this union between England, Scotland, Wales and Ireland was a new version of the official flag – the Union Flag. This is often called the Union Jack. The flag combined crosses associated with England, Scotland and Ireland. It is still used today as the official flag of the UK.

The Union Flag consists of three crosses:

- The cross of St George, patron saint of England, is a red cross on a white background.

- The cross of St Andrew, patron saint of Scotland, is a diagonal white cross on a blue background.

- The cross of St Patrick, patron saint of Ireland, is a diagonal red cross on a white background.

There is also an official Welsh flag, which shows a Welsh dragon. The Welsh dragon does not appear on the Union Flag; this is because the Principality of Wales was already united with England when the Union Flag was created – in 1606.

Now test out what you've learned, with our revision quiz! You'll find full mock tests at the back of this book!

Revision Quiz

Q1. What was the name of the first Prime Minister?

Q2. In 1746, Charles Stuart's rebel army was crushed. At which battle did this take place?

Q3. Name a famous work (often sung on New Year's Day) from the Scottish poet, Robert Burns.

Q4. What was the Industrial Revolution?

Q5. What were the downsides to the Industrial Revolution?

Q6. Who were the two main commanders in the Battle of Waterloo?

Q7. In 1833, which act abolished slavery in the British Empire?

Q8. What caused the War of Independence?

See the next page for the answers!

Answers

1. The name of the first Prime Minister was Robert Walpole.

2. The Battle of Culloden.

3. *Auld Lang Syne*.

4. The Industrial Revolution is the name for the rapid period of industrialisation that Britain went through, in the 18th and 19th centuries.

5. Working conditions were extremely dangerous. Young children were employed and worked unreasonable hours, there was no employee protection in place so employers could do whatever they liked.

6. Duke of Wellington and Napoleon

7. The Emancipation Act.

8. The British Government wanted to tax their North American colonies. The colonies objected to this and declared independence from Britain, who declared war on the colonies.

THE VICTORIAN AGE

In 1837, Queen Victoria ascended the throne. She was just 18 years old. Victoria reigned for 64 years, from 1837 until her death in 1901. She is one of the longest reigning British monarchs of all time, second only to the current Queen of England (2016) Elizabeth II. Victoria was an extremely popular monarch, and is remembered that way to this day. Under her rule, there were numerous social reforms, and Britain expanded its territory. The period during which she ruled became known as the Victorian Age.

Industry and Ireland

Under Victoria, Britain redoubled its efforts and became an even stronger trading nation. The government reduced taxes on imported goods. A good example of this was the repealing of the Corn Laws, in 1846. This made it easier to import cheap raw materials – such as grain – which in turn bolstered British industry.

In factories, working conditions became better, and laws were put in place to reduce the number of hours that women and children could work per day. In 1847, the number of hours that women and children could work was limited by law to 10 hours per day. Better housing also began to be built for workers.

The transport industry was also vastly improved. Prior to Victoria taking the throne, the first railway engine was created by George and Robert Stephenson; railway systems were consequently built throughout the British Empire. There were also great advances in other areas, such as the building of bridges by engineers such as Isambard Kingdom Brunel. Brunel was responsible for constructing the Great Western Railway, which was the first major railway built in Britain. It runs from Paddington Station in London to the south west of England, the West Midlands and Wales. Many of Brunel's bridges are still in use today.

British industry swiftly became the strongest in the world. More than half of the world's iron, coal and cotton was produced by the UK, which also acted as a financial hub for banks, insurance and business. Britain was booming. In 1851, the Great Exhibition opened in Hyde Park in Crystal Palace. This was a huge building, made of iron and glass. Exhibits ranged from huge machines to handmade goods. Countries from all over the world showed their goods, but most of the objects were made in Britain.

Unfortunately, Ireland did not fare as well as the rest of the UK. Over two thirds of the Irish population depended on farming, with potatoes forming a huge part of their diet. In the middle of the 19th century, Ireland suffered a major famine. Approximately 1 million people died from starvation and disease, and hundreds of thousands more left the country, emigrating to countries like the United States and Britain. The famine left many people in Ireland with a feeling of prolonged resentment towards the British government who they felt had not done enough to help. This resentment would boil over into the next century, and have a significant impact on the future of Ireland. The Irish nationalist movement began to grow, with groups such as the Fenians advocating for complete independence. Individuals like Charles Stuart Parnell advocated for 'Home Rule', where Ireland would have its own parliament but still remain in the UK.

The Empire

Under Victoria, Britain greatly expanded its territory, and eventually covered all of India, Australia and a huge portion of Africa. It became the largest empire in history, with over 400,000 million people living in British territories. Britain itself experienced an enormous amount of people coming in, and coming out. Over 13 million people left the country between the years of 1853-1913, but at the same time people continued to visit Britain from other countries. Many of these people came to Britain to escape persecution in their own countries; cities like London and Manchester became multi-cultural hubs.

The Crimean War

As ever, this period did not go without conflict. Between 1853 and 1856, Britain allied with Turkey and France amongst conflict with Russia. This developed into the Crimean War. The war was given unprecedented media coverage, with photographs and news stories of the war dominating press coverage. Unfortunately, this war laid bare the flaws in British medical care; many soldiers died from illnesses contracted in hospital rather than from actual war injuries. The Crimean War was also where the Victoria Cross medal originated from, with Queen Victoria awarding the medal to soldiers for bravery.

The Crimean War also gave centre stage to one of the most influential medical figures in British history – Florence Nightingale. Born in 1820, to English parents, Nightingale trained as a nurse in Germany before travelling to Turkey to treat soldiers fighting in the Crimean War. Her team of nurses significantly improved the mortality rate at the hospitals in which they were working. In 1860, she opened the Nightingale Training School for nurses in London. This was based at St Thomas' Hospital, and still exists to this day. Many of the nursing practices that Nightingale implemented are used in modern medical care; she is seen by many people as a founder of nursing.

Voting Rights

The Reform Act of 1832 had significantly increased the number of people who could vote. Pocket and rotten boroughs had been abolished, and more parliamentary seats were available than ever before to towns and cities. However, voting was still based on property ownership. The working class were unable to vote, and this led to a feeling of resentment. A group of campaigners, known as the Chartists, presented petitions to parliament, demanding the right to vote for the working class and for those who didn't own property. At first they seemed to be unsuccessful, but then another act was passed in 1867, lowering the amount of property that a person needed to be able to vote. However, it still left the majority of men without a vote, and women were excluded altogether.

Women's Rights

In 19th century Britain, women had significantly fewer rights than men. They could not vote, and when a woman got married, her earnings and property instantly belonged to her husband. In 1870 and 1882, acts were passed which gave married women the right to maintain their own earnings and property. Then, in the late 19th/early 20th century, women's suffrage movements began. These consisted of great numbers of women campaigning for better rights, and for the right to vote.

The suffragettes were led by Emmeline Pankhurst. After establishing the Women's Franchise League, which aimed to give married women a vote in local elections, she then founded the Women's Social and Political Union. This was the first time that the word 'suffragettes' was used. The group was highly controversial, and used antagonistic tactics to achieve results. They vandalised property, set fire to buildings and chained themselves to railings. Many of the group went on hunger strike.

In 1918, women over the age of 30 were given voting rights, and in 1928 women were given the right to vote from the age of 21 onwards. Whether the suffragettes were responsible for this is a hotly debated topic in historical circles. It is almost certainly true that the decision to give women voting rights, was largely down to female contributions during the First World War. Many people argue that the suffragettes actually damaged the argument for women's votes, although it is undeniable that they brought widespread attention to the cause, and in doing so had a significant impact.

The Decline of the Empire

The British Empire reached its peak during the Victorian Era, but in the late 19th century things started to change. While there was an enormous sense of pride in Britain, and a strong belief that the Empire was beneficial for the country; there were also concerns that the Empire had become too large to manage. Unnecessary conflicts in areas such as Africa and India accentuated this issue. Then, in 1899, Britain fought against the Netherlands in The Boer War. This brought the cost of war into the forefront of public minds. Many people died during the war, and the conflict also induced an outpouring of public sympathy for the Boer people; who were caught in the middle. Following this conflict, the Empire began a gradual wane, as more and more countries started to be granted their independence from Britain.

This period also saw the rise of one of the most famous writers – Rudyard Kipling. Born in India in 1865, Kipling wrote books and poems set in both India and the UK. His poems and novels reflected the idea that the British Empire was a force for good. He was awarded the Nobel Prize in Literature in 1907. His books included the *Just So Stories* and *The Jungle Book*, which continue to be popular today. His poem *If* has often been voted among the UK's favourite poems. It begins with these words:

> '*If you can keep your head when all about you*
> *Are losing theirs and blaming it on you;*
> *If you can trust yourself when all men doubt you,*
> *But make allowance for their doubting too;*
> *If you can wait and not be tired by waiting,*
> *Or being lied about, don't deal in lies.*
> *Or being hated, don't give way to hating,*
> *And yet don't look too good, nor talk too wise.'*
>
> (*If*, Rudyard Kipling)

Now test out what you've learned, with our revision quiz! You'll find full mock tests at the back of this book!

Revision Quiz

Q1. Queen Victoria is the longest serving monarch in British history. True or false?

Q2. Who created the first British railway engine?

Q3. Why were Ireland unable to reap the same reform benefits as England?

Q4. Between 1853 and 1856, Britain participated in which war?

Q5. Who was Florence Nightingale?

Q6. What did the Chartists want?

Q7. Who led the Suffragettes?

Q8. What tactics did the Suffragettes use to gain attention?

See the next page for the answers!

Answers

1. False. Queen Victoria is the second longest serving monarch in British history. Queen Elizabeth II is the longest.

2. George and Robert Stephenson.

3. In the middle of the 19th century, Ireland suffered a major famine, resulting in the deaths of approximately a million people.

4. The Crimean War.

5. Florence Nightingale was a nurse who worked during and after the Crimean War. She saved thousands of lives during the war, and had an enormous impact upon modern medicine.

6. The Chartists wanted the right to vote for the working class and for those who didn't own property.

7. The Suffragettes were led by Emmeline Pankhurst.

8. The Suffragettes used disruption tactics to get their message across. They vandalised property, set fire to buildings and chained themselves to railings. Many of them also went on hunger strike.

THE 20TH CENTURY

For Britain, it's fair to say that the 20th century was something of a mixed bag. While the century gave rise to some of the most important medical and technological advances in history, which have saved and changed millions of lives; the majority of the 100 years was dominated by international conflict and strife.

At the turn of the century, Britain was full of beans – a phrase which here means optimistic and positive. With the strongest Empire in history, the world's premier navy and a thriving industry, Britain was a major global heavyweight. At home, things were improving. Acts were passed which allowed for free school meals, pensions were introduced and more help was given to the unemployed. Laws were introduced to improve the safety of the workplace, and town planning rules were tightened to prevent further development of slums. Local government became more democratic and a salary for members of Parliament was introduced. Women's rights were improving too, with better support given to divorced wives.

World War One

Unfortunately, this didn't last. Events from abroad took a negative turn on the 28th June 1914, when Archduke Franz Ferdinand of Austria was assassinated. This sparked a chain reaction, which led to the outbreak of the First World War (1914-18). While the assassination was the trigger, there were a range of other factors in the build up to the event that made the ramifications much worse. Abroad, there was a heightened sense of nationalism from major European nations, and naturally this brought about increased militarism.

During the war, Britain formed part of the Allied Powers, with France, Russia, Japan, Belgium, Serbia and others. The entire British Empire fought during the war, with countries such as India fighting for Britain. The war was waged against the Central Powers of Germany, Austria-Hungary and Bulgaria. Millions of people died during the conflict. Britain itself lost 420,000 soldiers during the infamous Battle of the Somme, and over 2 million over the course of the war.

The First World War ended at 11am on the 11th November 1918, a date which is still commemorated to this day. Britain and her allies were the victors. Several months of post-war negotiation ended with Germany signing The Treaty of Versailles, in which (amongst other terms) they accepted total responsibility for the war, agreed to pay extensive reparation fees and surrender their land.

Irish Split

As mentioned, the turn of the century was an extremely positive time for Britain. With everything running so smoothly, in 1913 the British government passed a bill that would allow for 'Home Rule' in Ireland. This would mean that Ireland would be self-governed, and have its own parliament; but at the same time would still belong to the UK.

Unfortunately, the outbreak of the First World War forced the government to postpone the implementation of this. This caused great anger among Irish Nationalists; who responded by rebelling against the British. The rebellion culminated in the Easter Rising, where rebels fought for 6 days before surrendering. The leaders of the rebellion were executed.

After several further years of conflict, a peace treaty was signed in 1921. Then, in 1922, Ireland split into two countries. The northernmost 6 counties, which were Protestant, remained as part of the UK. This was named Northern Ireland. The rest of the country became the Irish Free State, and later became what is known as The Republic of Ireland. The split was not well received by everyone in Ireland, many of whom still wanted Ireland to be one nation – independent of Britain. This led to years of problems between Irish nationalists, Northern Ireland and the British government, commonly referred to as 'the Troubles'.

The 1920s

The 1920s were, for the most part, a positive time in British history. Although there was much rebuilding to be done after the war, Britain was aided by the boom in the USA and as a result, cities underwent vast improvement, and living conditions were bettered. However, in 1929 the world was plunged into the 'Great Depression'. Britain suffered heavily, with many areas of the country suffering from enormous rates of unemployment. Despite this, it wasn't all bad for Britain. While industries such as shipbuilding were hit extremely hard, newer industries – such as the automobile industry - developed and flourished. The fall in prices meant that those who hadn't lost their jobs had more money to spend on luxuries such as cars. New houses were built, and writers such as Graham Greene and Evelyn Waugh flourished. The economist John Maynard Keynes published influential new theories of economics.

This period also saw the development of the BBC as the world's first ever regular television service. This was aided by the development of the television, by Scottish born John Logie Baird. In the early 1930s, the first televised broadcast was made between London and Glasgow. During the same period, Alan Turing – a British mathematician, created the Turing machine. This has been instrumental in the development of modern computer science.

Now test out what you've learned, with our revision quiz! You'll find full mock tests at the back of this book.

Revision Quiz

Q1. Who did Britain ally with during the First World War?

Q2. During WWI, Britain lost 420,000 soldiers in a single battle. What was the name of this battle?

Q3. Why does Britain commemorate 11am, on the 11th November?

Q4. Following WWI, Germany was forced to sign which treaty?

Q5. What caused The Easter Rising?

Q6. In 1922, which key event occurred in Ireland?

Q7. What is the common name for the problems between Irish Nationalists and the British government?

Q8. In 1929, The Great Depression hit. Which aspect of British life was hit particularly hard by this?

See the next page for the answers!

Answers

1. During the First World War, Britain formed part of the Allied Powers with France, Russia, Japan, Belgium, Serbia and others.

2. The Battle of the Somme.

3. Britain commemorates this day/time as it is when the First World War finished, in 1918.

4. The Treaty of Versailles.

5. Irish Nationalists were furious at the postponement of a bill allowing for home rule in Ireland. They rebelled, with fatal consequences.

6. In 1922 Ireland split into two countries. The northernmost 6 counties, which were Protestant; remained as part of the UK. This was named Northern Ireland. The rest of the country became what is known as The Republic of Ireland.

7. The Troubles.

8. The Great Depression resulted in huge unemployment rates in Britain.

WORLD WAR TWO

Germany was hit extremely hard by the Great Depression. Already in enormous reparations debt to countries like the USA and France, the German economy took a ferocious battering. This boiled over into widespread public resentment of those who had inflicted the much-hated Treaty of Versailles – which the German people believed was unfair.

The atmosphere was ideal for political change. Thus, in 1933, Adolf Hitler was named Chancellor of Germany. Hitler seized on the German people's anger. He promised to tear up the Treaty of Versailles, take back the land that Germany had lost, and conquer new global territory. He immediately set about rebuilding the German army, which has been desolated by the treaty, and testing the resolve of Allies by invading other countries. Desperate to avoid another global conflict, Britain and France allowed Hitler numerous concessions. This culminated in the famous Munich Agreement, where Britain and France were forced into accepting an agreement with Hitler, to annexe portions of Czechoslovakia. Poland and Hungary seized on this, gobbling up Czech territories which they had previously fought for. Hitler swiftly broke his agreement, seizing the rest of Czechoslovakia, and then advancing into Poland in 1939. This was the final straw for Britain, who announced war.

World War 2 was initially fought between the Axis powers – consisting of Germany, Italy and Japan, and the Allies – consisting of Britain, France, Poland, New Zealand, Australia, South Africa and Canada. Hitler and his Nazi party began a racial campaign of extermination, and committed mass murder against groups that they deemed to be inferior in society. Millions of Jews were put to death in German concentration camps, and were joined by the disabled and by prisoners of war. In reality, this was just the start of Hitler's plan. Nazi plans for a German led post-war Europe included the complete and total extermination of all Slavic peoples, and would have generated death tolls that far exceeded anything seen in the war.

In 1940 a new British Prime Minister was declared – Winston Churchill. This changing of the guard would prove pivotal.

Winston Churchill

Winston Churchill is one of the most revered Prime Ministers in British history, and has even been voted as the greatest Briton of all time. His leadership during the Second World War was exemplary, and his refusal to surrender to Germany proved inspirational to British citizens. Although Churchill lost the General Election in 1945, he returned to work as Prime Minister in 1951, and then worked as an MP until 1964. He died in 1965, and was given a state funeral. Churchill is famous for his rousing, inspirational speeches – many of which you will still hear repeated today. These included lines such as:

'I have nothing to offer but blood, toil, tears and sweat.'

Churchill's first speech to the House of Commons after he became Prime Minister in 1940.

'We shall fight on the beaches,
We shall fight on the landing grounds,
We shall fight in the fields and in the streets,
We shall fight in the hills,
We shall never surrender.'

Speech to the House of Commons after Dunkirk in 1940.

'Never in the field of human conflict was so much owed
by so many to so few.'

Speech to the House of Commons during the Battle of Britain in 1940.

The Fall of France

In 1940, German forces defeated combined allied troops and successfully captured France. This was an enormous shock to Britain and the rest of the world, and a clear sign that Hitler was winning the war. Britain swiftly moved to evacuate both British and French troops from the beaches of Dunkirk. A huge number of civilian volunteers, many in tiny boats, contributed to the rescue of over 300,000 men. Although a huge number of lives were lost that day, the evacuation was considered a major success and had a moral boosting effect. However, with the fall of France, Britain stood almost alone against Germany until 1941 – when the USA entered the war.

The Battle of Britain

Britain was a top priority for Hitler. He wanted to invade, but – with Britain being an island – he first needed to control British airspace. The German's waged a fierce air campaign against Britain, but were defeated in what became known as the Battle of Britain, in 1940. The British used fighter planes such as the Hurricane and the Spitfire to repel the German Luftwaffe. Many historians see this event as a major turning point in the war, as it constituted Germany's first big defeat. Although they were defeated, and Hitler forced to postpone his invasion plans, Germany continued to bomb British cities such as London. This was named the Blitz, and resulted in a large number of deaths and structural damage. Cities such as Coventry were hit extremely hard by the bombings. Despite this, British people famously remained spirited and strong. The term 'Blitz spirit' is often used today to describe this attitude, and Britain often receives high praise from historians for the way in which the people reacted in the face of such adversity. It was not uncommon in this time period to hear people talking about the bombings in the same casual way that they would the weather, for example – 'it's been a touch Blitzy today.' At the same time as defending Britain, the British military was fighting the Axis on many other fronts. In Singapore, the Japanese defeated the British and then occupied Burma, threatening India.

The End of the War

Germany had allied with Japan. However, Japan made a colossal mistake in December 1941. After Japan bombed Pearl Harbour, the United States (who were previously neutral) were persuaded to enter the war. This would have enormous consequences.

In the meantime, Hitler was attempting to take Russia. This remains the largest invasion attempt in history, with an enormous portion of the German army being sent to Russia. The Eastern Front, as it became known, contributed to more deaths than any other element of WW2. Although Germany had enormous initial success, and seemed poised to topple Stalin (Russia's leader), they were ultimately defeated by a combination of poor weather and poor planning. Hitler had planned for a short, summer campaign, but the fighting went on well into the winter, slowing down the German offensive and giving Russian forces time to regroup.

To this day, historians are hugely divided over the role of Stalin and Russia in winning the war. Stalin's rapid industrialisation came at the cost of millions of innocent Russian lives. He was a genocidal monster. Although Germany underestimated Russia, and were often surprised by the quality of Russian tanks and weaponry, they had little trouble sweeping through Russian resistance until the weather turned on them, and it was the USA who ultimately provided the financial backing for Russia to succeed. To add to Russia's problems, in 1941 Stalin had purged the Red Army leadership, replacing them with barely competent generals, who were poorly placed to repel the Nazi threat.

That being said, there is no way that major battles such as Kursk or Stalingrad could have been won without the resistance that forced industrialisation provided the Russians, slowing the Germans down and significantly turning the tide of the war. Likewise, Stalin's policies ultimately gave the Soviets the military strength to march on Berlin, toppling Hitler in the process. The Soviet Union incurred astronomical casualties as a result of the Eastern Front, far exceeding the death toll of any other country (over 20 million deaths), but was absolutely pivotal in defeating Hitler.

This marked an uptrend in the allied forces fortunes. With the help of the USA, allied forces gradually started winning more and more battles. On the 6th June 1944, they arrived in Normandy. A fierce conflict was waged on the beaches, which the allies won. This is referred to as D-Day, and is regarded as one of the most crucial events of the war. It signalled the beginning of the allies taking back key territories from Germany.

Following this, allied forces moved on to recapture France and then to Germany itself. By May 1945, Germany had been defeated. Hitler and other top German leaders committed suicide to avoid capture, although many were put on trial and executed for their war crimes. In August 1945 Japan too was forced to surrender after the United States dropped atomic bombs on Hiroshima and Nagasaki. The war was over.

Now test out what you've learned, with our revision quiz! You'll find full mock tests at the back of this book.

Revision Quiz

Q1. How did Hitler persuade the people of Germany to vote for him?

Q2. Which two countries joined Hitler, in annexing areas of Czechoslovakia?

Q3. Which two elements led to the failure of Germany's invasion of Russia?

Q4. What does the term 'blitz spirit' refer to?

Q5. Name one type of British fighter plane that was used during WW2.

Q6. Which event persuaded the USA to get involved in the war?

Q7. Why is D-Day significant?

Q8. During World War 2, Italy was part of the Allied powers. True or False?

See the next page for the answers!

Answers

1. Hitler seized on the German people's anger. He promised to tear up the Treaty of Versailles, take back the land that Germany had lost, and conquer new global territory.

2. Hungary and Poland.

3. Poor planning and poor weather.

4. British optimism during WW2.

5. Hurricane.

6. The bombing of Pearl Harbour.

7. It signalled the beginning of the allied powers taking back territory from Germany.

8. False.

POST-WAR BRITAIN

Following the war, Britain began an extensive period of recovery. The nation had suffered economically during the war; people wanted a change. This led to the election of a Labour government in 1945. Clement Attlee took over as Prime Minister, and immediately began to implement wider social reforms as outlined by the Beveridge Report. This was a report created by William Beveridge, an economist and social reformer. The report recommended that the government should find ways of fighting the five 'Giant Evils' of Want, Disease, Ignorance, Squalor and Idleness.

Atlee had acted as Churchill's deputy during the war, and following this, led the party for 20 years. Under Atlee's government, working conditions were greatly improved. With the help of Aneurin Bevan, the Minister for Health, the NHS (National Health Service) was also established, guaranteeing a minimum standard of free healthcare for all British citizens. Atlee's government also introduced a benefits system, and nationalised industries such as coal mining, gas and railways.

In the meantime, Britain was also making important medical discoveries. In 1928, Scottish born doctor Alexander Fleming had discovered penicillin. By the 1940s, scientists Howard Florey and Ernst Chain had worked out how to use penicillin as medicine. This was quickly mass produced, and Fleming won the 1945 Nobel Prize in Medicine. In 1953, British scientists discovered the structure of the DNA molecule, which had enormous consequences for modern science.

The education system developed significantly during this period. Richard Austen Butler, a Conservative MP, became responsible for education in 1941. In this role, he oversaw the introduction of the Education Act in 1944. This introduced free secondary education in England and Wales. The education system has changed significantly since the Act was introduced, but the division between primary and secondary schools that it enforced still remains in most areas of Britain.

As mentioned earlier, the Empire had been on the wane for some time, and now Britain recognised the need for self-government in its former colonies. In 1947, 9 countries (including India and Pakistan) were granted independence from British rule; many other colonies followed suit over the next 2 decades.

Although the war was over, this did not put a stop to clashes between rival nations. The Soviet Union became the new threat for Britain and its allies. As a result of this threat, the North Atlantic Treaty Organisation (NATO) was set up, with the intent of resisting a potential invasion by the Soviet Union and its allies. Britain joined, and completed development of its own atomic bomb. The first test of this came in 1952, and was titled Operation Hurricane.

In 1951, Britain again had a Conservative government. This lasted until 1964, and represented a time of economic and social prosperity for British people. The Prime Minister of the day, Harold Macmillan, was famous for his 'wind of change' speech about decolonisation and independence for the countries of the Empire. However, there remained a significant shortage of labour. For this reason, the government began to encourage immigration; agents were sent abroad to recruit workers from overseas. The most popular recruitment countries were the West Indies, India and Pakistan, from which many citizens came to live and work in Britain.

The Swinging Sixties

The 1960s was a period of major social change in Britain. It was nicknamed the Swinging Sixties, after the development of fashion, music and cinema. Iconic bands such as The Beatles and The Rolling Stones captured the hearts of the nation, and consumerism was on the increase. The sixties also brought about a great deal of liberalisation for people in Britain. Women benefitted from this, gaining the right to equal pay, along with the abolishment of other sexist practices in the workplace. Meanwhile, Britain continued to develop technologically. Working together, Britain and France produced the first supersonic commercial airliner, which was named Concorde. The late sixties (1967) also saw the implementation of the first cash dispensing ATM, or 'cashpoint' as it's known today. This was created by James Goodfellow, and put into practice by Barclays Bank in north London.

The 60s were also famous for Roald Dahl. Dahl was born in Wales. He started publishing books during the 1940s, but it was during the 60s that his work really began to get noticed. Books such as *James and the Giant Peach, Charlie and the Chocolate Factory* and *Fantastic Mr Fox* were all published during this period, and Dahl's writing career extended all the way to the early 90s. Many of Roald Dahl's books have been made into films, and he is one of the most widely read authors of the 20th century.

Towards the end of the 60s, the number of people migrating from the West Indies, India, Pakistan and what is now Bangladesh fell. This was because the government passed new laws to restrict immigration. Immigrants were now required to have a strong connection to Britain through birth or ancestry. Even so, during the early 1970s, Britain admitted 28,000 people of Indian origin who had been forced to leave Uganda.

The 1970s

The late 70s saw an end to Britain's economic boom. As a result, prices rose sharply and the exchange rate became unstable. British industry was heavily impacted by this, and trade unions became more and more powerful. There was unrest between unions and the government, and strikes became prevalent. In 1972, the Northern Ireland Parliament was suspended, and the country was ruled by the UK government. This was combined with extreme violence from terrorist groups such as the Irish Republican Army (IRA), and many people lost their lives in the ensuing conflicts.

Margaret Thatcher

From 1979 till 1990, Britain was run by a Conservative government. Margaret Thatcher, Britain's first female Prime Minister, was at the head of this. Thatcher was the longest-serving Prime Minister of the 20th century, and stayed in office for 11 years. She introduced a number of reforms, whilst still maintaining a close relationship with the USA – then under the presidency of Ronald Reagan.

Thatcher's government re-privatised various nationalised industries and brought much sought-after restrictions to trade unions. Deregulation saw a great increase in the role of City of London as an international centre for investments, insurance and other financial services. In 1982, Britain fought Argentina for control of the Falkland Islands, a British owned territory. After a short military conflict, Britain was triumphant. This greatly increased the popularity of Thatcher. Following Thatcher, Britain was run by John Major.

Before we move onto the next section, let's look at some great British inventions of the 20th century!

Great British Inventions

The television was developed by Scotsman John Logie Baird in the 1920s. In 1932, he made the first television broadcast between London and Glasgow.

Radar was developed by Scotsman Sir Robert Watson-Watt, who proposed that enemy aircraft could be detected by radio waves. The first successful radar test took place in 1935. Working with radar led Sir Bernard Lovell to make new discoveries in astronomy. The radio telescope he built at Jodrell Bank in Cheshire was for many years the biggest in the world, and continues to operate today.

Insulin was co-discovered by John Macleod, and is used to treat diabetes.

The **Jet Engine** was developed in Britain during the 1930s by Sir Frank Whittle, a British Royal Air Force engineer officer.

The **Hovercraft** was invented by Sir Christopher Cockerell, during the 1950s.

The **Harrier Jump Jet** was designed and developed in the UK.

IVF (in-vitro fertilisation) therapy for the treatment of infertility was pioneered in Britain by physiologist Sir Robert Edwards and gynaecologist Patrick Steptoe. The world's first 'test-tube baby' was born in Oldham, Lancashire in 1978. In 1996, two British scientists – Sir Ian Wilmot and Keith Campbell led a team which was the first to succeed in cloning a mammal, Dolly the sheep.

MRI (magnetic resonance imaging) was co-invented by Sir Peter Mansfield, a British scientist. This enables doctors and researchers to obtain exact and non-invasive images of human internal organs.

The **World Wide Web** was invented by Sir Tim Berners-Lee, a British inventor.

Now test out what you've learned, with our revision quiz! You'll find full mock tests at the back of this book.

Revision Quiz

Q1. Why was the 1960s nicknamed 'the Swinging Sixties'?

Q2. During the 60s, Britain worked in collaboration with another country to produce the Concorde. Which country was this?

Q3. Who is Roald Dahl?

Q4. What was the name of Britain's first female prime minister?

Q5. Who did Britain fight for control of the Falklands Islands?

Q6. Who replaced Margaret Thatcher as Prime Minister?

Q7. In 1972, which governmental change took place in Northern Ireland?

Q8. Who was the longest serving British Prime Minister of the 20th century?

See the next page for the answers!

Answers

1. It was nicknamed the Swinging Sixties, after the development of fashion, music and cinema.

2. France.

3. Roald Dahl was one of the most influential authors of the 20th century. He wrote famous books like *James and the Giant Peach* and *Charlie and the Chocolate Factory.*

4. Margaret Thatcher.

5. Argentina.

6. John Major.

7. The Northern Ireland Parliament was suspended, and the country was run by the UK government.

8. Margaret Thatcher.

TONY BLAIR

In 1997, Tony Blair of the Labour Party was elected Prime Minister. The new Labour government created a Scottish Parliament and a Welsh Assembly. The Scottish Parliament has substantial powers to legislate. The Welsh Assembly was given fewer legislative powers but considerable control over public services. Blair's government also built on the Irish peace process that the previous Prime Minister, John Major, had started. This resulted in the Good Friday Agreement, signed in 1998. The Northern Ireland Assembly was elected in 1999 but suspended in 2002. It was not reinstated until 2007. Most paramilitary groups in Northern Ireland have decommissioned their arms and are inactive. Blair was replaced as Prime Minister in 2007 by Gordon Brown.

The 90s and 2000s have unfortunately been marked by significant conflict in the Middle East, with both Britain and the USA at the forefront of hostilities. Britain played a leading role in coalition forces involved in the liberation of Kuwait, following the Iraqi invasion in 1990, and the conflict in the Former Republic of Yugoslavia. Since 2000, British armed forces have been engaged in the global fight against international terrorism and against the proliferation of weapons of mass destruction, including operations in Afghanistan and Iraq. British combat troops left Iraq in 2009.

The UK now operates in Afghanistan as part of the United Nations mandated 50-nation International Security Assistance Force (ISAF) coalition, and at the invitation of the Afghan government. ISAF is working to ensure that Afghan territory can never again be used as a safe haven for international terrorism, where groups such as Al Qa'ida could plan attacks on the international community. As part of this, ISAF is building up the Afghan National Security Forces and is helping to create a secure environment in which governance and development can be extended.

2010 Onwards

In 2010, the results of the General Election yielded no overall majority. This meant that Britain became ruled by a Conservative and Liberal Democrat coalition, the first time such a government had been implemented since 1974. The leader of the Conservative Party, David Cameron, became Prime Minister. In 2015, the Conservative Party won the general election by a majority and thus the coalition was no more. However, Cameron was rocked by the results of the 2016 EU Referendum (which he had granted), where the people of Britain voted to leave the EU. As a consequence, he resigned shortly after, and Theresa May became the 2nd female Prime Minister of the United Kingdom.

Now test out what you've learned, with our revision quiz! You'll find full mock tests at the back of this book.

Revision Quiz

Q1. In 1997, Tony Blair was elected Prime Minister of Britain. What party did Tony Blair represent?

Q2. Tony Blair worked hard to repair relations with Irish rebellion groups. In 1998, his efforts culminated in which peace agreement?

Q3. Who replaced Tony Blair as Prime Minister?

Q4. Which country did Britain assist in the Iraq Invasion of 2003?

Q5. In 2010, Britain became ruled by a coalition between the Conservative Party and the Liberal Democrats. Why was this?

Q6. Why did David Cameron resign as Prime Minister, in 2016?

Q7. Who succeeded David Cameron as Prime Minister?

Q8. Theresa May was the third woman to become British Prime Minister, true or false?

See the next page for the answers!

Answers

1. The Labour Party.

2. The Good Friday Agreement.

3. Gordon Brown.

4. America.

5. The results of the general election produced no majority decision.

6. David Cameron resigned due to the result of the EU Referendum, where the people of Britain voted to leave the EU.

7. Theresa May.

8. False, she is the second.

MODERN DAY
BRITAIN

In order to become a British citizen, and integrate into British society, it's important that you have a sustained knowledge of present-day Britain, along with some of the most essential UK traditions and customs. In this section, we'll explain everything you need to know about present-day Britain.

THE UK POPULATION

The UK is a multicultural hub. Post-war immigration means that nearly 10% of the population has a parent or grandparent born outside of the UK. The population of the UK has grown extremely fast in recent years. This is down to elements such as longer life expectancy, increased migration and better living. Britain has a record number of elderly citizens.

In terms of diversity, Britain attracts people from all over the world. This is strongest in major cities, such as London. While the most common ethnicity of people in the UK is white, Britain is also home to many people of Asian, black and mixed descent.

Despite this variation, the UK's population is highly uneven in terms of distribution. England has approximately 84% of the total population, with the rest being made up by Scotland, Wales and finally Northern Ireland.

With such diversity, Britain has various equality laws which must be followed. It is illegal to discriminate in the UK; both men and women have equal rights to work, own property and marry. If they are married, both parents are equally responsible for their children.

Officially, women are given exactly the same rights as men, and work within all sectors of the economy, making up approximately half of the entire workforce. On average, girls leave school with better qualifications than boys. On top of this, more women than men now study at university. The past view of women having to stay at home is (officially) considered outdated and sexist; there are far greater employment opportunities for women than in the past. You will find women working in all sectors of the economy; many of whom are operating as senior managers in traditionally male-dominated occupations.

LANGUAGE

The UK contains a number of different accents, dialects and languages. The language spoken and the accent/dialect used will vary depending on where you are. In Wales, the language primarily spoken in some parts of the country is Welsh. This is a completely separate language to English, and is taught in schools and universities throughout Wales. However, the vast majority of Welsh people use English as their most common spoken language. In some parts of Scotland, Gaelic – another separate language, is spoken. Northern Ireland contains a mixture of Irish Gaelic and English.

CURRENCY

The main bank in the UK is known as the Bank of England. Britain uses a currency known as the British Pound; this is the oldest currency that is still in use today. Other names for the British Pound include the Pound Sterling, Sterling and Quid. If you need to convert Euros into British pounds, then you can do this via the post office. This applies for any other currency too but you should be aware that less used currencies may require time for processing. The denominations of currency in the UK are as follows:

Coins: 1p, 2p, 5p, 10p, 20p, 50p, £1 and £2

Notes: £5, £10, £20, £50

Northern Ireland and Scotland have their own banknotes, which are valid everywhere in the UK. However, shops and businesses do not have to accept them.

GEOGRAPHY OF THE UK

Geographically, the UK is situated in North West Europe. Britain has a number of key towns and cities, but a larger portion of Britain consists of countryside. People from inside towns and cities frequently use the countryside for holidays or leisure breaks, as they are perfect for activities such as walking and camping. The longest distance on the mainland is from John O'Groats on the north coast of Scotland, to Land's End in the south-west corner of England. It is about 870 miles (approximately 1,400 kilometres).

On the next few pages, we've broken down the UK into different maps, to show you each country and the cities that belong to it.

Here you can see a map of the entire UK; with England, Scotland, Wales and Northern Ireland visible. You can also see the Republic of Ireland.

And below, the counties of Wales, along with the major cities:

1 BLAENAU GWENT
2 BRIDGEND
3 CAERPHILLY
4 MERTHYR TYDFIL
5 NEATH PORT TALBOT
6 RHONDDA CYNON TAFF
7 SWANSEA
8 TORFAEN
9 VALE OF GLAMORGAN

And finally, the counties of Northern Ireland, along with the major cities:

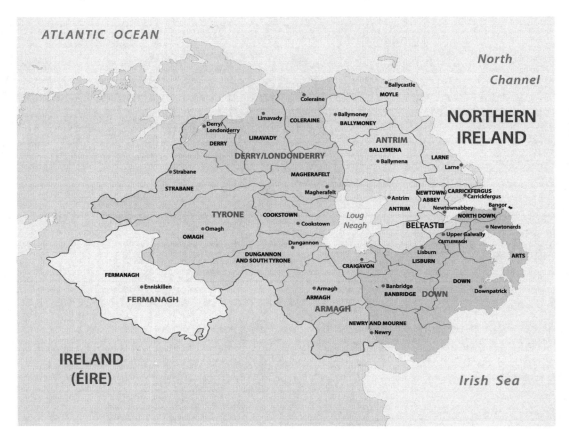

RELIGION

As you have probably gathered from reading the prior section of this book, England has a deep religious history. In the 2009 Citizenship Survey, 70% of people identified themselves as Christian. Muslims (4%), Hindus (2%), Sikhs (1%), Jews and Buddhists (0.5%) make up a much smaller part of the population. Despite the smaller proportion, England contains a large number of religious buildings to accommodate for other religions than Christianity, such as Islamic mosques, Jewish synagogues, and Sikh gurdwaras. In the UK, approximately 21% of people identify themselves as atheist.

In England, the Church and the state are constitutionally linked. The official Church of the state is the Church of England (called the Anglican Church in other countries and the Episcopal Church in Scotland and the United States). It is a Protestant Church and has existed since the Reformation in the 1530s.

The monarch is the head of the Church, and the Archbishop of Canterbury is the spiritual leader of the Church. The Archbishop is generally selected by the Prime Minister and a Church-based committee, but the Monarch also has the right to select the Archbishop if they wish. Several Church of England bishops sit in the House of Lords.

England also contains other Protestant groups, such as Quakers and Methodists, and also still has a very large Roman Catholic following.

Scotland uses a slightly different system, in that the national church is a Presbyterian Church – the Church of Scotland. This is governed by ministers and elders. The chairperson of the General Assembly of the Church of Scotland is the Moderator, who is appointed for one year only and often speaks on behalf of that Church. Wales and Northern Ireland do not have an established Church.

Religious Festivals

As the UK is strongly Christian, there are a number of religious festivals held, which you will need to be aware of when living here. Below we have laid out these events and the dates on which they are held, in full:

- **Christmas Day.**

Christmas Day is on the 25th December, and celebrates the birth of Jesus Christ. It is a public holiday, and is traditionally celebrated by eating a special meal (normally involving turkey), giving gifts and decorating houses. Many people have a decorated tree in their home. Religious people attend church on Christmas Eve (24th December), or on Christmas Day, whilst young children are taught that Father Christmas brings them presents the night before. All in all, Christmas Day is a very special time in the UK.

- **Boxing Day.**

Boxing Day is the day after Christmas Day. It is named after a historical tradition (no longer in place) where servants and tradesmen would receive presents from their employers or customers. In the UK, Boxing Day is a public holiday.

- **Easter.**

Easter takes place in March or April, depending on where the moon is in its cycle. The day marks the rising of Jesus from the dead, on Easter Sunday, after his death on Good Friday. Both Good Friday and the Monday after Easter, known as Easter Monday, are public holidays.

Prior to Easter, Christians take a period of 40 days to reflect and prepare. This is known as Lent. During Lent, many people give up something important to them (such as their favourite food) to reflect the sacrifice that Jesus made. The day before Lent is known as Shrove Tuesday/Pancake Day. People traditionally use this day to eat pancakes and other foods that they intend to give up before fasting for Lent. Lent begins on Ash Wednesday. There are church services where Christians are marked with an ash cross on their forehead as a symbol of death and sorrow for sin.

Easter is not only celebrated by religious people, but by non-religious people too. Chocolate eggs are traditionally given as a gift on Easter Day, to symbolise new life.

As mentioned, the UK is not just home to Christians. Many other religions exist within the UK, and have their own festivals. Below we have listed some of these:

- **Diwali.**

Diwali is celebrated by both Hindus and Sikhs. It is known as the Festival of Lights, and celebrates the triumph of good over evil, and the gaining of knowledge. The festival lasts for 5 days, and is traditionally celebrated in October or November. There are many different stories about how the festival came about. There is a famous celebration of Diwali in Leicester.

- **Hanukkah**.

Hanukkah is a Jewish festival, and is held in November or December. It lasts for 8 days, and commemorates the Jews' struggle for religious freedom. On each day of the festival, a candle is lit on a stand of eight candles (called a menorah) to remember the story of the festival, where oil that should have lasted only a day did so for eight.

- **Eid al-Fitr.**

Eid al-Fitr is a Muslim festival that is held to celebrate the end of Ramadan, when Muslims have fasted for a month. They thank Allah for giving them the strength to complete the fast. The date when it takes place changes every year. Muslims attend special services and meals.

- **Eid ul Adha**

Eid ul Adha remembers that the prophet Ibrahim was willing to sacrifice his own son when God ordered him to. It reminds Muslims of their own commitment to God. Many Muslims sacrifice an animal to eat during this festival. In Britain, this has to be done in a slaughterhouse.

- **Vaisakhi.**

Vaisakhi is a Sikh festival, celebrating the founding of the Khalsa – the Sikh Community. It is held on April 14th every year, and celebrated with parades, dancing and singing.

Other Traditions

Along with all of the aforementioned, Britain also has plenty of non-religious traditions. These include:

- **New Year.**

The New Year is a major event, and is celebrated on the night of 31st December (New Year's Eve) and the day of 1st January (New Year's Day). In Scotland, New Year's Eve is known as Hogmanay, and the 2nd of January is a public holiday. For some Scottish people, Hogmanay is a bigger holiday than Christmas.

- **Valentine's Day.**

Valentine's Day is on the 14th February. It is a day where lovers exchange cards and romantic gifts. Sometimes people send anonymous cards to someone they secretly admire.

- **April Fool's Day.**

April Fool's Day is on the 1st April, and lasts until 12 midday. During this time, people play jokes on each other, and you'll often find that newspapers and websites publish fake stories, designed to amuse and catch you out.

- **Mother's Day.**

Mother's Day (or Mothering Sunday) takes place three Sundays before Easter. On this day, children buy gifts for their mothers.

- **Father's Day.**

Father's Day takes place on the third Sunday in June. On this day, children buy gifts for their fathers.

- **Halloween.**

Halloween is celebrated on the 31st October. It is celebrated by dressing up in frightening costumes, laying out spooky decorations (such as pumpkins) and playing 'trick or treat'. People often have Halloween parties to celebrate.

- **Bonfire Night.**

Bonfire Night is celebrated on the 5th November. On Bonfire Night, people set off fireworks at home or attend firework displays, where an effigy of a 'guy' is burned. The origin of this event goes back to 1605, where a group of Catholics attempted to kill the Protestant king, by blowing up the Houses of Parliament. They failed. Although people remember Guy Fawkes, the conspirator assigned to light the bomb fuse, Guy Fawkes was not actually the leader of the conspirators. This was Robert Catesby.

- **Remembrance Day.**

Remembrance Day is on the 11th November, and commemorates all of those who have died fighting for Britain and its allies in war. The day was originally created to remember the victims of World War One, which ended on the 11th November 1918, at 11am. As a mark of respect, people wear poppies (the red flower found on the battlefields of the First World War) and hold a two-minute silence. At 11am, there is a two-minute silence and wreaths are laid at the Cenotaph in Whitehall, London.

PATRON SAINTS' DAYS

In the UK, each of the countries has a special day, dedicated to a national saint. These are as follows:

- St David's Day, Wales: 1st March
- St Patrick's Day, Northern Ireland: 17th March
- St George's Day, England: 23rd April
- St Andrew's Day, Scotland: 30th November

Both Scotland and Northern Ireland have a public holiday on their patron saint's day. While England and Wales do not have public holidays to celebrate, they do still commemorate the event, with small festivals and parades being held to mark the occasion.

Along with the above celebrations, the UK also has a number of public holidays each year. These are known as bank holidays. During these days, banks and most other businesses are closed. These days are of no religious significance. They are at the beginning of May, in late May or early June, and in August. In Northern Ireland, the anniversary of the Battle of the Boyne in July is also a public holiday.

Now test out what you've learned, with our revision quiz! You'll find full mock tests at the back of this book.

Revision Quiz

Q1. Approximately what percent of the current UK population have ancestors who were born outside of Britain?

Q2. Which country within the UK has the highest number of people living in it?

Q3. Whereabouts in Europe is the UK situated?

Q4. What is the most popular religion within the UK?

Q5. The Monarch does not have the right to select the Archbishop of Canterbury. True or False?

Q6. On which date is Christmas Day celebrated?

Q7. List 3 other non-Christian festivals that take place in the UK.

Q8. Which Patron Saint's Day takes place on the 23rd April?

See the next page for the answers!

Answers

1. 10%.

2. England.

3. Geographically, the UK is situated in North West Europe.

4. Christianity.

5. False.

6. 25th December.

7. Eid-Al-Fitr, Diwali, Hanukkah.

8. St George's Day.

MUSIC

Music in Britain has a rich heritage, and plays a really important part in British culture. Britain is home to all kinds of music, from pop to rock, jazz to classical. Every year, a huge range of big musical events take place across the UK.

Classical music is really popular in the UK, and events such as The Proms are indicative of this. The Proms is an eight-week summer season of orchestral classical music, which takes place in various venues, including the Royal Albert Hall in London. It has been organised by the British Broadcasting Corporation (BBC) since 1927. The Last Night of the Proms is the most well-known concert and (along with others in the series) is broadcast on television.

Classical music has been popular in the UK for many centuries. Henry Purcell (1659-95) was the organist at Westminster Abbey. He wrote church music, operas and other pieces, and developed a British style distinct from that elsewhere in Europe. He continues to be influential on British composers.

Other important composers include:

- **George Frederick Handel** (1685-1759), who spent many years in the UK and became a British citizen in 1727. He wrote the *Water Music* for King George I and *Music for the Royal Fireworks* for his son, George II. Both of these pieces continue to be very popular. Handel also wrote an oratorio, *Messiah*, which is sung regularly by choirs, often at Easter time.

- **Gustav Holt** (1874-1934), whose work includes *The Planets*, a suite of pieces themed around the planets of the solar system. He adapted *Jupiter*, part of the Planet's suite, as the tune for *I vow to thee my country*, a popular hymn in British churches.

- **Sir Edwar Elgar** (1857-1934) was born in Worcester, England. His best-known work is probably the *Pomp and Circumstance Marches. March No 1 (Land of Hope and Glory)* is usually played at the Last Night of the Proms at the Royal Albert Hall.

- **Ralph Vaughan Williams** (1872-1958) wrote music for orchestras and choirs. He was strongly influenced by traditional English folk music.

- **Sir William Walton** (1902-83) wrote a wide range of music, from film scores to opera. He wrote marches for the coronations of King George VI and Queen Elizabeth II, but his best known works are probably *Façade*, which became a ballet, and *Belshazzar's Feast*, which is intended to be sung by a large choir.

- **Benjamin Britten** (1913-76) is best known for his operas, which include *Peter Grimes* and *Billy Budd*. He also wrote *A Young Person's Guide to the Orchestra*, which is based on a piece of music by Purcell and introduces the listener to the various different sections of an orchestra. He founded the Aldeburgh festival in Suffolk, which continues to be a popular music event of international importance.

The Royal Albert Hall

Other types of popular music, including folk music, jazz, pop and rock music have flourished in Britain since the 20th century. Britain has had a huge impact on popular music around the world, due to the wide use of the English language, the UK's cultural links with many countries, and British capacity for invention and innovation.

Since the 1960s, British pop music has made one of the most important cultural contributions to life in the UK. Bands including The Beatles and The Rolling Stones continue to have an influence on music both here and abroad. British pop music has continued to innovate. For example, the Punk movement of the late 1970s and the trend towards boy and girl bands in the 1990s.

There are many large venues that host music events throughout the year, such as: Wembley Stadium, the O2 in Greenwich, south-east London, and the Scottish Exhibition and Conference Centre (SECC) in Glasgow.

Festival season in the UK takes place in the summer, with major events in various locations. Famous festivals include Glastonbury, the Isle of Wight Festival, and the Reading and Leeds Festivals. Many bands and solo artists, both well-known and up-and-coming, perform at these events.

The National Eisteddfod of Wales is an annual cultural festival which includes music, dance, art and original performances largely in Welsh. It includes a number of important competitions for Welsh poetry.

For British artists, the rewards and recognition are plentiful. Every September, the best album of the year from the UK and Ireland is awarded with the Mercury Music Prize, the 2016 recipient was grime icon Skepta. Furthermore, the prestigious Brit Awards are held annually, and deliver a range of prizes for artists; such as awarding the best British solo artist and group.

FILMS

The UK has had an enormous impact on modern cinema. From 1896 onwards, when the first public film screening was shown, Britain became a major film nation. Early British film makers were innovative and daring, and became associated with using unique and clever special effects in their films. British actors such as Charlie Chaplin dominated the silent movie market; Chaplin was one of the first British actors to make the move to Hollywood.

During the 1930s, British movies were used as a way of boosting wartime morale. British studios flourished during this period, and directors such as Sir Alexander Korda and Sir Alfred Hitchcock came to prominence. Later, directors like Ridley Scott – who directed films such as *Alien* and *Gladiator* – found success both in the UK and internationally. During the 1950s and 1960s, British comedies such as *Passport to Pimlico, The Ladykillers* and later, the *Carry On* films, were hugely successful.

Britain continues to produce high-grossing films, with franchises such as *Harry Potter* and *James Bond* being amongst the foremost of these. Many of the films now produced in the UK are made by foreign companies, using British expertise. Ealing Studios has a claim to being the oldest continuously working film studio facility in the world. Britain continues to be particularly strong in special effects and animation. One example is the work of Nick Park, who has won four Oscars for his animated films, including three for films featuring *Wallace and Gromit*.

In terms of actors, Britain also boasts an impressive array. Actors such as Kate Winslet, Colin Firth, Sir Anthony Hopkins and Dame Judi Dench have all made their mark on the global stage, winning Oscars for their performances. Every year, the British Academy of Film and Television Arts hosts the BAFTA awards, which reward outstanding British actors. This is the British equivalent of the Oscars.

Famous British films include:

- *The 39 Steps* (1935), directed by Alfred Hitchcock
- *Brief Encounter* (1945), directed by David Lean
- *The Third Man* (1949), directed by Carol Reed
- *The Belles of St Trinian's* (1954), directed by Frank Launder
- *Lawrence of Arabia* (1962), directed by David Lean
- *Women in Love* (1969), directed by Ken Russell
- *Don't Look Now* (1973), directed by Nicolas Roeg
- *Chariots of Fire* (1981), directed by Hugh Hudson
- *The Killing Fields* (1984), directed by Roland Joffe
- *Four Weddings and a Funeral* (1994), directed by Mike Newell
- *Touching the Void* (2003), directed by Kevin MacDonald

TV

Television in the UK is extremely popular, and there are a huge variety of channels to choose from. You will find that some of these are free to watch, whilst others will require you to pay a subscription fee. Amongst the most popular television programmes in the UK are soap operas, such as *Coronation Street, Eastenders* and *Emmerdale*. These are generally shown throughout the week, during the evening, and centre on issues such as family, relationships, drugs and sometimes murder. In Scotland, some Scotland-specific programmes are shown and there is also a channel with programmes in the Gaelic language. There is a Welsh-language channel in Wales. There are also programmes specific to Northern Ireland and some programmes broadcast in Irish Gaelic.

Television comedy also has its own style. The tradition of comedy and satire, and the ability to laugh at ourselves, are an important part of the UK character. Medieval kings and rich nobles had jesters who told jokes and made fun of people in the Court. Later, Shakespeare included comic characters in his plays. In the 18th century, political cartoons attacking prominent politicians – and sometimes the monarch or other members of the Royal Family – became increasingly popular. In the 19th century, satirical magazines began to be published. The most famous of these was *Punch*, which was published for the first time in the 1840s. Today, political cartoons continue to be published in newspapers and magazines such as *Private Eye*.

In the UK, television directors have used the above to create situation comedies, or sitcoms, which often look at family life and relationships in the workplace. These are extremely popular. Satire has also continued to be important, with shows like *That Was The Week That Was* in the 1960s and *Spitting Image* in the 1980s and 90s. In 1969, *Monty Python's Flying Circus* introduced a new type of progressive comedy – stand-up comedy. This is where a solo comedian talks to a live audience. Often, these performances are recorded and played back on TV channels in the UK.

In order to watch TV in the UK, you must have a television license. This applies even if you are watching TV on a computer, or on any other medium. A single TV license can be used to cover all of the equipment in one house, however if you are renting different rooms in a shared house (with a separate tenancy agreement) then you will each need a separate license. If you are over the age of 75, then you are eligible to apply for a free license, and blind people receive 50% off the price. The punishment for watching TV without a license is severe, and can go up to fines of £1000. The money that you pay for your TV license goes towards the British Broadcasting Corporation (BBC). The BBC is a public service, which provides television and radio programmes; it is the largest broadcaster in the entire world, and operates independent of the government. Provided you own a television license, the BBC is completely free to use. Unlike other TV channels, the BBC is not funded through advertisements and subscriptions.

BBC radio stations are also funded by TV licenses. There are many different radio stations in the UK. Some of these broadcast nationally, and others only broadcast in certain cities or regions. There are radio stations that play certain types of music and some broadcast in regional languages such as Welsh or Gaelic. Similarly to the BBC TV channels, BBC radio stations are not funded through advertisements and subscriptions; but via TV licenses.

Now test out what you've learned, with our revision quiz! You'll find full mock tests at the back of this book.

Revision Quiz

Q1. What is 'The Proms'?

Q2. When is the festival season in the UK?

Q3. Name two historically influential British bands.

Q4. Name two famous British directors.

Q5. What are the BAFTA awards?

Q6. What is a soap opera?

Q7. What does the money from a Television License go towards?

Q8. It is a legal requirement to have a television license if you live in the UK. True or false?

See the next page for the answers!

Answers

1. An 8 week orchestral music extravaganza.

2. During the summer.

3. The Beatles and The Rolling Stones.

4. Alfred Hitchcock and Ridley Scott.

5. The BAFTAs are the British equivalent of the Oscars, and reward outstanding British actors.

6. A soap opera is a television show which centres on issues such as family, relationships, drugs and sometimes murder.

7. The money from television licenses goes towards the British Broadcasting Corporation (BBC). The BBC is a public service, which provides television and radio programmes; it is the largest broadcaster in the entire world.

8. False. It is only a legal requirement to have a television license in the UK if you are watching TV.

THEATRE

As we discussed in the history section of this guide, theatre is a huge part of British culture. With playwrights such as Shakespeare embedded in British history, it goes without saying that Britain is a country of theatre lovers. Most towns and cities in the UK have some form of theatre. London's West End, also known as 'Theatreland' is particularly well known. *The Mousetrap*, a murder-mystery play by Dame Agatha Christie, has been running in the West End since 1952 and has had the longest initial run of any show in history.

There is also a strong tradition of musical theatre in the UK. In the 19th century, Gilbert and Sullivan wrote comic operas, often making fun of popular culture and politics. These operas include *HMS Pinafore, The Pirates of Penzance* and *The Mikado*. Gilbert and Sullivan's work is still often staged by professional and amateur groups. More recently, Andrew Lloyd Webber has written the music for shows which have been popular throughout the world, including, in collaboration with Tim Rice, *Jesus Christ Superstar* and *Evita,* and also *Cats* and *The Phantom of the Opera.*

Along with theatre productions, Britain also has a long tradition of pantomime. Pantomime, often shortened to 'panto', is a type of musical comedy performed on stage. These comedies are often based on fairy stories and are light-hearted, with music and comedy, to be enjoyed by family audiences. One of the traditional characters is the Dame, a woman played by a man. There is also often a pantomime horse or cow played by two actors in the same costume.

The Edinburgh Festival takes places in Edinburgh, Scotland, every summer. It consists of a series of different arts and cultural festivals, with the biggest and most well-known being the Edinburgh Festival Fringe ('The Fringe'). The Fringe is a showcase of mainly theatre and comedy performances. It often shows experimental work.

Similarly to the music awards, British theatre has its own awards every year. These are named the Laurence Olivier Awards and take place at various places in London. Categories such as best actor, best actress and best director are awarded. It is considered highly prestigious to win such an award, which is named after the late Sir Laurence Olivier, who participated in various Shakespeare plays.

LITERATURE AND POETRY

The UK is steeped in literary history, and some of the most influential writers in history have come from Britain. A number of British writers have won the Nobel Prize in Literature, including the likes of William Golding and Harold Pinter. British writers have produced work that is revered and read across the world, with authors such as Ian Fleming (the creator of *James Bond*), JRR Tolkien *(The Lord of the Rings)* and Agatha Christie (writer of murder mysteries) having an enormous global impact. In 2003, *The Lord of The Rings* was voted the country's best loved novel. Other famous British writers include:

- **Jane Austen** (1775-1817) is a famous English novelist, and the author of books such as *Pride and Prejudice* and *Sense and Sensibility.* Jane Austen's work is focused on the theme of marriage and relationships, and many of her works have been produced for television and film.

- **Charles Dickens** (1812-70) is famous for writing novels such as *Oliver Twist, Bleak House* and *Great Expectations*. He is widely considered to be the greatest novelist of the entire Victorian Era, and it is possible to hear references in everyday talk to some of the characters in his books, such as Scrooge (a mean person) or Mr Micawber (always hopeful).

- **Robert Louis Stevenson** (1850-94) wrote books which are still read by adults and children today. His most famous books include: *Treasure Island, Kidnapped* and *Dr Jekyll and Mr Hyde.*

- **Thomas Hardy** (1840-1928) was an author and poet. His best-known novels focus on rural society and include *Far from the Madding Crowd* and *Jude the Obscure.*

- **Sir Arthur Conan Doyle** (1859-1930) was a Scottish writer, who produced the world famous stories of *Sherlock Holmes*. He is considered to be a pioneer of detective fiction.

- **Evelyn Waugh** (1903-66) wrote satirical novels, including *Decline and Fall* and *Scoop*. He is perhaps best known for *Brideshead Revisited.*

- **Sir Kingsley Amis** (1922-95) was an English novelist and poet. He wrote more than 20 novels. The most well-known of these is *Lucky Jims.*

- **Graham Greene** (1904-91) wrote novels often influenced by his religious beliefs, including *The Heart of the Matter, The Honorary Consul, Brighton Rock* and *Our Man in Havana.*

- **J K Rowling** (1965-) is the author of the *Harry Potter* children's books, which have gone to produce enormous global success. She also writes crime fiction for adults.

Every year, the Man Booker Prize for Fiction is awarded for the best original novel. While this was previously only open to candidates from the Commonwealth, Ireland and Zimbabwe, it has recently been extended to include any English language novel. It has been in existence since 1968. Past winners include Ian McEwan, Hilary Mantel and Julian Barnes.

Along with fiction writing, Britain also has a strong history of poetry. The Anglo-Saxon poem *Beowulf* tells of its hero's battles against monsters and is still translated into modern English. Poems which survive from the Middle Ages include Chaucer's *Canterbury Tales* and a poem called *Sir Gawain and the Green Knight,* about one of the knights at the court of King Arthur.

As well as plays, Shakespeare wrote many sonnets (poems which must be 14 lines long) and some longer poems. As Protestant ideas spread, a number of poets wrote poems inspired by their religious views. One of these was John Milton, who wrote *Paradise Lost.*

Other poets, including William Wordsworth, were inspired by nature. Sir Walter Scott wrote poems inspired by Scotland and the traditional stories and songs from the area on the borders of Scotland and England. He also wrote novels, many of which were set in Scotland.

Poetry was especially popular during the 19th century, with poets such as William Blake, John Keats, Lord Byron, Percy Shelley, Alfred Lord Tennyson, and Robert and Elizabeth Browning. Later, many poets – for example, Wilfred Owen and Siegfried Sassoon – were inspired to write about their experiences in the First World War. More recently, popular poets have included Sir Walter de la Mare, John Masefield, Sir John Betjeman and Ted Hughes.

Some of the best-known poets are buried or commemorated in Poet's Corner in Westminster Abbey.

Some famous lines include:

'Oh, to be in England now that April's there,
And whoever wakes in England sees, some morning, unaware,
That the lowest boughs and the brushwood sheaf,
Round the elm-tree bole are in tiny leaf,
While the Chaffinch sings on the orchard bough,
In England – Now!'

(Robert Browning – *Home Thoughts from Abroad*)

'She walks in beauty, like the night,
Of cloudless climes and starry skies;
And all that's best of dark and bright,
Meet in her aspect and her eyes.'

(Lord Byron – *She Walks in Beauty*)

'Tyger! Tyger! Burning bright,
In the forests of the night,
What immortal hand or eye,
Could frame thy fearful symmetry?'

(William Blake – *The Tyger*)

'What passing-bells for these who die as cattle?
Only the monstrous anger of the guns.
Only the stuttering rifles' rapid rattle,
Can patter out their hasty orisons.'

(Wilfred Owen – *Anthem for Doomed Youth*)

Although poetry is now arguably on the decline, poems by the aforementioned writers are commonly studied in schools and university programmes, and make up an essential part of students' education programme.

ART AND FASHION

Over the years, Britain has produced some of the most outstanding art in the world. British art started out with mostly religious themes, consisting of paintings in churches and drawings in religious books. Much of this was lost after the Protestant Reformation, but wealthy families began to collect other paintings and sculptures. Many of the painters working in Britain in the 16th and 17th centuries were from abroad – for example, Hans Holbein and Sir Anthony Van Dyck. British artists, particularly those painting portraits and landscapes, became well known from the 18th century onwards.

Today, Britain is home to a number of highly impressive art galleries. The National Gallery and Tate Britain are in London, Cardiff has the National Museum and Edinburgh has the National Gallery of Scotland.

The Tate Britain Art Gallery in London

Notable British artists include:

- **Thomas Gainsborough** (1727-88) was a portrait painter who often painted people in country or garden scenery.

- **David Allan** (1744-96) was a Scottish painter who was best known for painting portraits. One of his most famous works is called *The Origin of Painting.*

- **Joseph Turner** (1775-1851) was an influential landscape painter in a modern style. He is considered the artist who raised the profile of landscape painting.

- **The Pre-Raphaelites** were an important group of artists in the second half of the 19th century. They painted detailed pictures on religious or literary themes in bright colours. The group included artists such as Holman Hunt, Dante Gabriel Rossetti and Sir John Millais.

- **Sir John Lavery** (1856-1941) was a very successful Northern Irish portrait painter. His work included painting the Royal Family.

- **Henry Moore** (1898-1986) was an English sculptor and artist. He is best known for his large bronze abstract sculptures.

- **John Petts** (1914-91) was a Welsh artist, best known for his engravings and stained glass.

- **Lucian Freud** (1922-2011) was a German-born British artist. He is best known for his portraits.

- **David Hockney** (1937) was an important contributor to the 'pop art' movement of the 1960s and continues to be influential today.

Britain awards contemporary artists with the Turner Prize. This was named after Joseph Turner, an influential landscape artist. There are four pieces of art shortlisted every year, and shown at Tate Britain, before the winner is announced. The Turner Prize is considered to be one of the most prestigious art awards in Europe. Previous winners include Richard Wright and Damien Hirst.

Britain doesn't just have great art, but it also has a rich heritage in fashion. Britain has contributed hugely to the industry, with iconic designers such as Alexander McQueen and Vivienne Westwood originating from the UK. Twice a year, London Fashion Week takes place, and this is considered to be one of the 'Big Four' world fashion weeks. It happens in February and again in September. Along with this, Britain has also produced other fantastic designers, such as Thomas Chippendale – who designed furniture in the 18th century, Clarice Cliff – who designed Art Deco ceramics, and Sir Terence Conran – a 20th century interior designer.

ARCHITECTURE

The architectural heritage of the UK is rich and varied. In the Middle Ages, great cathedrals and churches were built, many of which still stand today. Examples are the cathedrals in Durham, Lincoln, Canterbury and Salisbury. The White Tower in the Tower of London is an example of a Norman castle keep, built on the orders of William the Conqueror.

Gradually, as the countryside became more peaceful and landowners became richer, the houses of the wealthy became more elaborate and great country houses such as Hardwick Hall in Derbyshire were built. British styles of architecture began to evolve.

In the 17th century, Inigo Jones took inspiration from classical architecture to design the Queen's House at Greenwich and the Banqueting House in Whitehall in London. Later in the century, Sir Christopher Wren helped develop a British version of the ornate styles popular in Europe, shown in buildings such as the new St Paul's Cathedral.

In the 18th century, simpler designs became popular. The Scottish architect Robert Adam influenced the development of architecture in the UK, Europe and America. He designed the inside decoration as well as the building itself, in great houses such as Dumfries House in Scotland. His ideas influenced architects in cities such as Bath, where the Royal Crescent was built.

In the 19th century, the medieval 'gothic' style became popular again. As cities expanded, many great public buildings were built in this style. The Houses of Parliament and St Pancras Station were built at this time, as were the town halls in cities such as Manchester and Sheffield.

In the 20th century, Sir Edwin Lutyens had an influence throughout the British Empire. He designed New Delhi to be the seat of government in India. After the First World War, he was responsible for many war memorials throughout the world, including the Cenotaph in Whitehall. The Cenotaph is the site of the annual Remembrance Day Service attended by the Queen, politicians and foreign ambassadors.

Modern British architects include Sir Norman Foster, Lord Richard Rogers and Dame Zaha Hadid, whose work can be seen throughout the world, as well as within the UK.

Alongside the development of architecture, garden design and landscaping have also played an important role in the UK. In the 18th century, Lancelot 'Capability' Brown designed the grounds around country houses so that the landscape appeared to be natural, with grass, trees and lakes. Later, Gertrude Jekyll often worked with Edwin Lutyens to design colourful gardens around the houses he designed. Gardens continue to be an important part of homes in the UK. The annual Chelsea Flower Show showcases garden design from Britain and around the world.

Now test out what you've learned, with our revision quiz! You'll find full mock tests at the back of this book.

Revision Quiz

Q1. What is Panto?

Q2. Which British author wrote the *Lord of the Rings* series?

Q3. In which period did Charles Dickens write?

Q4. Who is JK Rowling?

Q5. Name a famous British fashion designer.

Q6. How many times a year does London Fashion Week take place?

Q7. Name two influential British artists.

Q8. Where can you find The National Gallery of Scotland?

See the next page for the answers!

Answers

1. Panto is the short term for pantomime. This is a type of musical comedy that is performed on stage.

2. JRR Tolkien.

3. The Victorian Era.

4. The author of the *Harry Potter* series.

5. Alexander McQueen.

6. Two times, in February and September.

7. Henry Moore and Lucian Freud.

8. Edinburgh.

SPORT

Sport is a really big deal in the UK. Although it's obviously not a necessity, it's important to understand that sport plays a massive part in British culture. Britain invented many of the most popular sports in the world, with games such as cricket, tennis, rugby, golf and football (even though they aren't much good at it) originating from the UK.

Throughout the country there are enormous stadiums to host sporting events. These include Wembley Stadium in London, Old Trafford (Manchester), Anfield (Liverpool), White Hart Lane (Tottenham) and the Millennium Stadium (Cardiff). The majority of towns, and every single city, will have sports facilities for the public such as tennis courts, gymnasiums or swimming pools. Britain has always played an important part in global sporting events; hosting the Olympic Games on three separate occasions: 1907, 1948 and 2012. The main Olympic site for the 2012 Games was in Stratford, East London. The British team was very successful during this event, finishing third in the overall medal table. Britain also hosted the 2012 Paralympic Games. The Paralympics have their origin in the work of Dr Sir Ludwig Guttman, a German refugee, at the Stoke Mandeville hospital in Buckinghamshire. Dr Guttman developed new methods of treatment for people with spinal injuries and encouraged patients to take part in exercise and sport.

The sports practised in Britain include:

- **Football**

Football is the most popular sport in the UK, and plays an important part in British culture. England, Scotland, Wales and Northern Ireland all have their own professional leagues; the most famous of these being the English Premier League. This is by far the richest league in the world, and attracts many of the world's best players and managers.

Globally, many UK teams compete in European competitions such as the UEFA Champions League and Europa League. Furthermore, almost every town and city in the UK has at least one professional club, which people from that town take great pride in supporting. England, Scotland, Wales and Northern Ireland all also have their own national football teams, which compete in international football competitions with other nations.

At Euro 2016, 3 of the home nations reached the group stage of the competition for the first time ever. Although Scotland did not qualify, for England, Wales and Northern Ireland this was a fantastic achievement. England's victory at the World Cup of 1966 remains the only international cup win between the 4 nations.

On an amateur and recreational level, football is extremely popular within the UK, and there are often people found playing the sport, every week, in parks and gardens across the country.

- **Cricket**

Cricket was invented in England, but has spread to many other countries. Cricket is a fairly complex game, which can last for up to 5 days and still result in a draw. Cricket is traditionally seen as a 'gentleman's game', where those playing are expected to demonstrate good sportsmanship and a spirit of fair play, which in itself is seen as an extension of the British character. Cricket terms such as 'rain stopped play', 'batting on a sticky wicket', 'playing a straight bat', 'bowled a googly', or 'it's just not cricket', have passed in everyday usage.

England has a highly successful cricket team, which competes against other international sides, and against Australia in the Ashes – a famous series of Test matches.

- **Rugby**

Rugby is another sport that was invented in England, and remains very popular in the country today. There are two different forms of rugby: union and league. Each of these forms have different rules, and there are separate leagues for each form in England, Wales, Scotland and Northern Ireland. Teams from all countries compete in a range of competitions. The most famous rugby union competition is the Six Nations Championship between England, Ireland, Scotland, Wales, France and Italy. The Super League is the most well-known rugby league (club) competition.

- **Horse Racing**

Horse Racing is historically popular in Britain, and is arguably the oldest of all these sports. The sport has a long association with royalty, and there are racecourses all over the UK. Famous horse-racing events include: Royal Ascot, a five-day race meeting in Berkshire attended by members of the Royal Family, the Grand National at Aintree near Liverpool, and the Scottish Grand National at Ayr. There is a National Horseracing Museum in Newmarket, Suffolk.

- **Golf**

The modern game of golf can be traced back to 15th century Scotland. It is a popular sport played socially as well as professionally. There are public and private golf courses all over the UK. St Andrews in Scotland is known as the home of golf. The Open Championship is the only 'Major' tournament held outside the United States. It is hosted by a different golf course every year.

- **Tennis**

Tennis is especially popular in England, where the first tennis club was founded in 1872, at Leamington Spa. Every year, Britain hosts The Wimbledon Championships. This is considered by many people to be the biggest tennis major of the calendar. It takes place at the All England Lawn Tennis and Croquet Club. Wimbledon is the oldest tennis tournament in existence, and remains the only 'Grand Slam' which is played on grass.

- **Water sports**

Sailing continues to be popular in the UK, reflecting our maritime heritage. A British sailor, Sir Francis Chichester, was the first person to sail single-handed around the world, passing the Cape of Good Hope (Africa) and Cape Horn (South America), in 1966/67. Two years later, Sir Robin Knox-Johnston became the first person to do this without stopping. Many sailing events are held throughout the UK, the most famous of which is at Cowes on the Isle of Wight.

Rowing is also popular, both as a leisure activity and as a competitive sport. There is a popular yearly race on the Thames between Oxford and Cambridge Universities.

- **Motor Sport**

Britain has a long history of producing great motor sport drivers, in both cars and motorbike racing. Britain is a world-leader in the development of motor-sport technology, and there are currently two British owned teams in the Formula 1 Championships: Williams and McLaren. Along with this, Britain also has the famous Silverstone racing track. The UK has produced a number of Championship winning drivers in the past, with the likes of Nigel Mansell, Jenson Button and Lewis Hamilton all taking home the championship.

- **Skiing**

Skiing is increasingly popular in the UK. Many people go abroad to ski, and there are also dry ski slopes throughout the UK. Skiing on snow may also be possible during the winter. There are five ski centres in Scotland, as well as Europe's longest dry ski slope, near Edinburgh.

Given Britain's sporting pedigree, it makes sense that the country has produced a number of notable sportsmen and women over the years. These include:

- **Sir Roger Bannister** (1929 –) was the first man ever to run a mile in under four minutes, in 1954.

- **Sir Jacket Stewart** (1939 –) is a Scottish former racing driver who won the Formula 1 world championship three times.

- **Bobby Moore** (1941-93) captained the World Cup winning English football team, in 1966. He is considered one of the greatest footballers in history.

- **Sir Ian Botham** (1955 –) captained the English cricket team and holds a number of English Test cricket records, both for batting and for bowling.

- **Jayne Torvill** (1957 –) and **Christopher Dean** (1958 –) won gold medals for ice dancing at the Olympics Games in 1984 and in four consecutive world championships.

- **Sir Steve Redgrave** (1962 –) won gold medals in five consecutive Olympic Games, for rowing. He is one of Britain's most decorated Olympians.

- **Baroness Tanni Grey-Thompson** (1969 –) is an athlete who uses a wheelchair and won 16 Paralympic medals, including 11 gold medals, in races over five Paralympic Games. She won the London Marathon six times, and broke a total of 30 world records.

- **Dame Kelly Holmes** (1970 –) won gold twice, for running in the 2004 Olympic Games. She holds a number of records.

- **Dame Ellen MacArthur** (1976 –) is a yachtswoman who became the fastest person to sail around the world on her own, in 2004.

- **Sir Chris Hoy** (1976 –) is a Scottish cyclist who has won six gold and one silver Olympic medals. He has also won 11 world championship titles.

- **Phil Taylor** (1960 –) is by far and away the most successful darts player of all time, and is widely considered to be the greatest darts player in history. He has a record of 16 World Championships, with 8 consecutive titles from 1995 till 2002.

- **David Weir** (1979 –) is a Paralympian who uses a wheelchair and has won six gold medals over two Paralympic Games. He has also won the London Marathon six times.

- **Sir Bradley Wiggins** (1980 –) is a cyclist. In 2012, he became the first Briton to win the Tour de France. He has won seven Olympic medals, including gold medals in the 2004, 2008 and 2012 Olympic Games.

- **Mo Farah** (1983 –) is a British distance runner, born in Somalia. He won gold medals in the 2012 Olympics for the 5,000 and 10,000 metres and is the first Briton to win the Olympic gold medal in the 10,000 metres.

- **Jessica Ennis** (1986 –) is an athlete. She won the 2012 Olympic gold medal in the heptathlon, which includes seven different track and field events. She also holds a number of British athletics records.

- **Andy Murray** (1987 –) is a Scottish tennis player, and the only British man to win a singles title in a Grand Slam since 1936 – in 2012, he won the men's singles in the US open. Murray has won Olympic gold twice, and has also won Wimbledon twice.

- **Ellie Simmonds** (1994 –) is a Paralympian who won gold medals for swimming at the 2008 and 2012 Paralympic Games. She holds a number of world records. She was the youngest member of the British team at the 2008 games.

Now test out what you've learned, with our revision quiz! You'll find full mock tests at the back of this book.

Revision Quiz

Q1. Name 2 famous British sporting stadiums.

Q2. In 2012, Britain hosted which major sporting event?

Q3. What is the most popular sport in the UK?

Q4. The English Premier League is the 2nd richest league in the world. True or false?

Q5. Which of the home nations did not qualify for Euro 2016?

Q6. Which popular horse racing event takes place at Aintree?

Q7. Which famous Grand Slam Tennis tournament is held in England every year?

Q8. Name 3 historically successful British sportspeople.

See the next page for the answers!

Answers

1. Wembley Stadium and Anfield.

2. The Paralympic Games.

3. Football.

4. False. The English Premier League is the richest.

5. Scotland.

6. The Grand National.

7. Wimbledon.

8. Andy Murray, Steve Redgrave, Roger Moore.

SOCIAL ACTIVITIES

In the UK, there are a variety of ways in which you can spend your free time. These include:

- **Social networking**

Social networking is enormous in the UK, and the vast majority of people use some form of networking site (such as Facebook and Twitter) to stay in contact with their friends, organise events and share things. It's extremely common to see people social networking even whilst out, by using their phones or other technology.

- **Pubs**

Going to the pub is something of a British tradition, and pubs are an integral element of UK culture. It is common to meet friends at the pub, where a number of activities are arranged and take place. Amongst these are events such as pub quizzes, games of pool or darts. Naturally, pubs serve alcohol, but you must be 18 or older to purchase this. If a person is 16 years old, they are permitted to remain in the pub but only with an adult supervisor/someone aged 18 or older. This extends to drinking too. Pubs are generally open from 11am, and most must stop serving alcohol at 11pm. Bars and nightclubs with dancing and music usually open and close later than pubs.

- **Gambling**

Gambling is very popular in Britain, and there are numerous casinos and betting shops across the country. In order to enter one of these premises, you must be 18 or older. Like many countries, the UK has a National Lottery, with draws being made every week. You must be 16 or older to participate in the National Lottery, which involves buying a ticket or scratch card from a shop or online.

- **Sports clubs**

As mentioned, there are many amateur sports clubs in the UK, and this is a great way to interact with and meet people. It is almost guaranteed that there will be some kind of sporting club or group near where you are living. Sports are one of the most popular general hobbies in the UK.

- **TV & video gaming**

The UK is one of the richest countries in the world, so people living in Britain have access to the most high-tech entertainment systems (provided they have the money, of course). Video gaming is extremely popular in the UK, and in many places there are video gaming meet-ups and clubs dedicated to playing. This is a very common way to spend your time. Likewise, with the sheer variety of television channels on offer, you are almost guaranteed never to be bored in your own home!

- **Pets**

Many people in the UK have some kind of pet, whether this is a cat, a dog or something more exotic. Reasons for this vary, but most of the time it's because the owners enjoy having them for company. It is against UK law to treat a pet with cruelty, likewise neglect is also illegal. Pet owners are held responsible for the behaviour of their pet. For example, if a dog goes to the toilet in a public place, the owner will be expected to clean it up. The UK has a really high standard of veterinary care, although these treatments are often expensive. In the UK, various charities exist which can sometimes help owners that cannot afford veterinary care.

- **Gardening**

Gardening is really popular in the UK, and a lot of people have gardens at home and will spend their free time looking after them. Some people rent additional land called 'an allotment', where they grow fruit and vegetables. Gardening and flower shows range from major national exhibitions to small local events. Many towns have garden centres selling plants and gardening equipment. There are famous gardens to visit throughout the UK, including Kew Gardens, Sissinghurst and Hidcote in England, Crathes Castle and Inveraray Castle in Scotland, Bodnant Gardan in Wales, and Mount Stewart in Northern Ireland.

The countries that make up the UK all have flowers which are particularly associated with them and which are sometimes worn on national saints' days:

- England – the rose
- Scotland – the thistle

- Wales – the daffodil

- Northern Ireland – the shamrock

- **Shopping**

There are many different places to go shopping in the UK. Most towns and cities have a central shopping area, which is called the town centre. Shopping centres are also common – these might be in town centres or on the outskirts of a town or city. Most shops in the UK are open seven days a week, although trading hours on Sundays and public holidays are generally reduced. Many towns also have markets on one or more days a week, where stallholders sell a variety of goods.

- **Cooking and food**

Many people in the UK enjoy cooking. They often invite each other to their homes for dinner. A wide variety of food is eaten in the UK because of the country's rich cultural heritage and diverse population.

There are a variety of foods that are traditionally associated with different parts of the UK:

- **England.** Roast Beef, which is served with potatoes, vegetables, Yorkshire puddings (batter that is baked in the oven) and other accompaniments. Fish and chips are also popular.

- **Wales.** Welsh cakes – a traditional Welsh snack made from flour, dried fruits and spices, and served either hot or cold.

- **Scotland.** Haggis – a sheep's stomach stuffed with offal, suet, onions and oatmeal.

- **Northern Ireland.** Ulster Fry – a fried meal with bacon, eggs, sausages, black pudding, white pudding, tomatoes, mushrooms, soda bread and potato bread.

- **Visiting places of interest.**

The UK is a tourism hotspot, and for good reason. It has an enormous number of exciting locations.

In the countryside, there are numerous opportunities for activities such as mountain biking or hill walking, and the UK also contains 15 national parks. Important areas of the countryside are maintained and kept open by the National Trust, which also works to preserve important buildings and coastal locations. The National Trust is a voluntary organisation, with over 62,000 members.

Likewise, in UK cities, there are also exciting places to visit. The UK has a huge number of museums, containing historical collections, and various landmarks are dotted all over the country, for example Big Ben. The majority of these landmarks are open to the public, although you will normally have to pay a fee to truly experience them.

On the next few pages, we've listed some popular places of interest in the UK:

<u>Edinburgh Castle</u>

Quick Facts

- Edinburgh Castle is built upon Castle Rock, part of an ancient volcano.

- While the exact date of when the castle was built is unknown, it is believed to have been constructed during the 12th century.

- The castle was an important royal site during the reign of Malcolm III and his son, King Edgar.

- During the 12th century, ownership of Edinburgh Castle changed twice: from Scotland to England and then back again!

- The castle has been used as a prison on a number of occasions. It was first used during the 18th and 19th century, and then again during World War I. It was also used as an arsenal to make weapons/ammunition during the 15th century.

- The castle of Edinburgh is one of Scotland's biggest tourist attractions.

London Eye

Quick Facts

- The London Eye is an enormous Ferris wheel, and stands at 443 feet tall. It is situated on the south bank of the River Thames.

- It takes around 30 minutes to complete a full revolution on the London Eye. Every revolution can carry up to 800 people.

- The London Eye is used by over 3 million people every single year. It contains 32 capsules, which can carry up to 25 people. There is space in the capsules for walking around and observation.

- The London Eye is often lit up in different colours, depending on world events. For example, it was lit up in the colours of the Union Jack, to celebrate the wedding of Prince William and Kate Middleton.

The Tower of London

Quick Facts

- The Tower of London was built by William the Conqueror, following his successful invasion in 1066. It was originally built as a royal palace and military stronghold.

- The Crown Jewels are kept in a vault at the Tower of London. The total value of the jewels exceeds £20 billion.

- The tower is a designated World Heritage Site, awarded by UNESCO. It is one of very few fully intact medieval buildings.

- Despite the tower's bloody reputation, only a small number of people have been executed at the tower. The last person to be executed at the tower was a German spy, in 1941.

- The Tower of London is said to be haunted by a number of medieval ghosts, amongst them Henry VI and Catherine Howard.

Snowdonia

Quick Facts

- Snowdonia is a national park, located in Wales. It is best known for being the home of Mount Snowdon – the highest mountain in Wales.

- Snowdonia covers an area of 838 square miles.

- The park is split into four main areas: the tourist area, the peaks, the remote area and the south.

- Roughly 350,000 people climb Snowdonia, and reach the summit, every single year!

- On average, it takes around 5/6 hours to scale and descend Snowdonia.

Wembley Stadium

Quick Facts

- Wembley Stadium is one of the most famous football stadiums in the world. It is located in north London, and can seat 90,000 people.

- Wembley was originally opened in 1923, but was later demolished and rebuilt in 2003.

- Wembley is the venue of the FA Cup Final, and has also played host to the UEFA Champions League Final on a number of occasions. FC Barcelona have played in 2 finals at Wembley, and won both.

- The Wembley Arch is 440 feet high, and spans over 1000 feet. Due to the height of the arch, it has beacons in place to warn low flying planes!

Big Ben

Quick Facts

- Big Ben is the name for the great bell of the clock at the eastern end of the Houses of Parliament, in London. Both the bell and the clock are commonly referred to, collectively, as Big Ben. It is a major British tourist attraction.

- The clock is over 150 years old. It was built between 1843 and 1858, and is 316 feet high.

- Although members of the public are not allowed inside the building without special permission, you can get a fantastic view of the clock from the London Eye.

- The minute hand on Big Ben weighs 220 pounds. Every year, the hand travels approximately 118 miles.

- The bell itself is over seven feet tall, and weighs almost the same as an elephant!

- During WWII, the sound of the bells chiming were broadcast, to show the world that Britain was still standing and had not been defeated.

<u>Loch Ness</u>

Quick Facts

- Loch Ness is located in the Highlands of Scotland. It is the second largest lake in Scotland, and reaches depths of 750 feet.

- The loch is famous for sightings of a legendary monster, named Nessie, which many people believe to reside within the lake. Since the 6th century, there have been numerous people claiming to see the beast, with some even producing (grainy) photographic evidence.

- Loch Ness contains more fresh water than all of the lakes in England and Wales combined. It is part of the Caledonian Canal, which connects Inverness to Fort William.

- There have been numerous attempts from researchers and scientists to prove (or disprove) the existence of Nessie. Searchers have used equipment such as cameras, fish bait and submarines, but have had no luck.

The Eden Project

Quick Facts

- The Eden Project is located in Cornwall. It contains biomes (giant greenhouses) and houses plants from all over the world.

- The Eden Project was opened in March 2001. By June 2001, it had already had one million visitors.

- The greenhouses of the Eden Project contain over 100,000 plants, representing over 5,000 species from all over the world.

- The Eden Project has a number of on-site facilities for visitors, including restaurants, gift shops and cafes.

- The Eden Project is often used as a venue for concerts, environmental conferences and even has an ice rink in the winter.

Now test out what you've learned, with our revision quiz! You'll find full mock tests at the back of this book.

Revision Quiz

Q1. How old do you need to be to purchase alcohol in a pub?

Q2. What is the minimum age requirement to participate in the National Lottery?

Q3. What is the National Trust?

Q4. Where in London can you find Big Ben?

Q5. Loch Ness is the biggest lake in Scotland. True or false?

Q6. Where in England is the Eden Project?

Q7. Where are the Crown Jewels kept?

Q8. How long does it take to complete a full revolution on the London Eye?

See the next page for the answers!

Answers

1. 18 years old or older.

2. 16 years or older.

3. The National Trust is a voluntary organisation which works to preserve important buildings and coastlines.

4. Big Ben can be found at the eastern end of the Houses of Parliament.

5. False. Loch Ness is the second largest lake in Scotland.

6. Cornwall.

7. The Tower of London.

8. 30 minutes.

THE UK GOVERNMENT

In order to be accepted as a British citizen, it is important that you have a good understanding of the UK Government and how it operates. This doesn't mean you need to get involved in heated political debates, but Britain is a democracy, this means that every single adult person plays a role. In this section, we'll look at how the British democratic system functions.

The Role of the Monarch

Queen Elizabeth II is the current monarch/head of state in the UK, and for many of the countries in the Commonwealth. She has reigned since 1952, and is the longest serving monarch in British history. In 2012, she celebrated her Diamond Jubilee (60 years as queen). She is married to Prince Philip, the Duke of Edinburgh, and her eldest son Prince Charles (the Prince of Wales) is the heir to the throne.

The UK operates under a constitutional monarchy. This means that the monarch does not rule the country. However, they are in charge of appointing a public-elected government. The monarch invites the leader of the party with the largest number of MPs, or more than one party, to become the Prime Minister. The monarch regularly meets with the Prime Minister, and can advise on laws/policies, but there is generally an understanding that the monarch won't get involved in the running of the country; decisions on government policies will be made by the Prime Minister and their cabinet.

The Queen has an important role to play. Foremost, she is an ambassador for the UK, and represents the country to the rest of the world. She entertains foreign ambassadors visiting the country, meets with heads of state and travels abroad, strengthening the UK's international relations. She is a figure of stability, national identity and pride for the British people who throw huge parties to celebrate her birthday and key anniversaries. The Queen also acts as an opener of ceremonies. Every year, she opens the new parliamentary session, summarising the government's aims and policies for the year to come. As part of your citizenship ceremony, you will need to swear loyalty to the Queen, repeating either the oath of allegiance (if you are religious) or the affirmation of allegiance (if you aren't religious).

The oath of allegiance is as follows:

'I (name) swear by Almighty God that on becoming a British citizen, I will be faithful and bear true allegiance to Her Majesty Queen Elizabeth the Second, her Heirs and Successors, according to law.'

The affirmation of allegiance is as follows:

'I (name) do solemnly, sincerely and truly declare and affirm that on becoming a British citizen, I will be faithful and bear true allegiance to Her Majesty Queen Elizabeth the Second, her Heirs and Successors, according to the law.'

In recognition of the monarch, the National Anthem of the United Kingdom is 'God Save The Queen'. This song is played during important occasions, and during the start of many sporting events. In order to become a British citizen, it's important that you learn the lyrics to the first verse of this song.

The National Anthem is as follows:

'God save our gracious Queen,
Long live our noble Queen,
God save the Queen!
Send her victorious,
Happy and glorious,
Long to reign over us,
God save the Queen!

O lord God arise,
Scatter our enemies,
And make them fall!
Confound their knavish tricks,
Confuse their politics,
On you our hopes we fix,
God save the Queen!

Not in this land alone,
But be God's mercies known,
From shore to shore!
Lord make the nations see,
That men should brothers be,
And form one family,
The wide world ov'er

From every latent foe,
From the assassins blow,
God save the Queen!
O'er her thine arm extend,
For Britain's sake defend,
Our mother, prince, and friend,
God save the Queen!

Thy choicest gifts in store,
On her be pleased to pour,
Long may she reign!
May she defend our laws,
And ever give us cause,
To sing with heart and voice,
God save the Queen!'

British Democracy

Democracy refers to a system of a government where every member of the adult population is given the right to influence national decisions, by voting in elections.

Although Britain is today a democracy, it hasn't always been that way. While parliament existed, only a small group of people could vote on who belonged to it – men who were 21 years or older and who owned property amounting to a certain value. As the 19th century progressed, this expanded to include more and more ordinary men and women. This was helped by the Chartists, who campaigned for governmental reform.

Amongst other things, the Chartists demanded:

- That every man should have the right to vote.

- That every region should have an equal say in the electoral system.

- That every man should be able to run for MP, and that MPs should be paid.

Although these demands were not well received initially, by 1918 the majority of them had been accepted. Women over 30 received the right to vote, and this was extended in 1928 to include men and women over the age of 21. In 1969, the voting age was changed, so that anyone who was 18 years or older could vote.

The Constitution

A constitution refers to a set of principles by which a country is run. The constitution includes laws and conventions, and ensures that those running the country behave responsibly and ethically. In Britain, the constitution is not written down. This is because Britain has never had any revolution or uprising which required the government to do so. In countries such as the USA, the constitution is written down and often referred back to in government. In Britain, the constitution could more accurately be described as an unwritten set of guidelines. Our most important institutions have developed over hundreds of years. There is mixed opinion in Britain over whether these should be written down in a full document, or whether an unwritten constitution is beneficial – as it allows the government more flexibility.

In Britain, the main constitutional institutions are:

- The Monarchy

- The Prime Minister

- Parliament

- The cabinet

- The judiciary

- The civil service

Along with this, the police and the local government also play an important role.

The Government

Britain is currently governed by the Conservative Party. The UK Government is separated into parliamentary constituencies. A constituency is a small area of the country. From each constituency, voters choose an MP to represent them in the House of Commons. Each MP belongs to a particular party, and the party with the majority of MPs then forms the government. In the event that voters don't reach a majority decision, two parties form a coalition.

The main parties of the UK are:

- The Conservative Party

- The Labour Party

- The Liberal Democrats

- The Green Party

- UKIP (UK Independence Party)

- The SNP (Scottish National Party)

Now, let's look at the role of some of the most important members of government:

- **The Prime Minister**

The Prime Minister is the leader of the governing party in power. This person appoints members of the cabinet and exercises control over other public appointments. The Prime Minister lives in 10 Downing Street, near the Houses of Parliament. The Prime Minister can be forced to resign if the MPs in his/her party decide they need a change, or if the Prime Minister themselves wishes to step down. Likewise, they will generally resign in the event of their party losing a General Election.

The current Prime Minister of the UK (2016) is Theresa May. She is only the second ever female Prime Minister. She assumed office on 13th July 2016.

- **The Cabinet**

Around 20 MPs are appointed by the Prime Minister, to act as ministers in charge of essential departments. As well as the minister, the department also has a number of other ministers, who are responsible for managing particular areas in the department.

Amongst these ministers are:

- o **The Chancellor of the Exchequer.** This person is responsible for the economy.

- o **The Home Secretary.** This person is responsible for crime and policing, as well as immigration matters.

The ministers chosen by the Prime Minister form a cabinet, who hold weekly meetings and make decisions about how to run the country. These decisions are then debated in parliament.

In the history section of this guide, we briefly touched upon the House of Commons and the House of Lords. Now, let's look at them in more detail:

The House of Commons

The House of Commons plays a more important role in Parliament than the House of Lords, because its members are elected democratically. The Prime Minister is a member of the House of Commons, as is his cabinet. In the House of Commons, each MP represents a specific parliamentary constituency, which is a small area of the country.

Amongst other things, MPs:

- Help with the creation and implementation of new laws.

- Debate with other members of government on essential national issues.

- Represent the needs of the people in their constituency.

The chief officer of the House of Commons acts as the 'Speaker' during debates. This means that they chair debates, and must remain neutral, even though they themselves are an MP who represents a constituency. Their role is to keep order during debates, make sure debate rules are followed and that both sides get a fair chance to speak. The Speaker is chosen via secret ballot, by the other MPs.

The House of Lords

Members of the House of Lords, known as peers, are not elected by the people and do not represent a constituency. The role and membership of the House of Lords has changed over the last 50 years.

Until 1958, all peers were:

- 'Hereditary' which means they inherited their title, or

- Senior judges, or

- Bishops of the Church of England

Since 1958, the Prime Minister has had the power to nominate peers just for their own lifetime. These are called life peers. They have usually had an important career in politics, business, law or another profession. Life peers are appointed by the monarch on advice of the Prime Minister. They also include people nominated by the leaders of the other main political parties or by an independent Appointments Commission for non-party peers.

Since 1999, hereditary peers have lost the automatic right to attend the House of Lords. They now elect a few of their number to represent them in the House of Lords.

The House of Lords is normally more independent of the government than the House of Commons. It can suggest amendments or propose new laws, which are then discussed by MPs. The House of Lords checks laws that have been passed by the House of Commons, to ensure that they are fit for purpose. It also holds the government to account, to make sure that it is working in the best interests of the people. There are peers who are specialists in particular areas, and their knowledge is useful in making and checking laws. The House of Commons has powers to overrule the House of Lords, but these are not used often.

If you wish to visit the House of Commons, or The House of Lords, and listen to debates in the public galleries; then you'll need to contact your local MP in advance. Alternatively, you can queue up on the day – outside of the building, to get in. Entrance is free but you can expect to be waiting a long time for entry.

The Houses of Parliament, Westminster

European Parliament

The EU also has a parliament, known as the European Parliament. Elections for this are held every five years, with members being known as MEPs. Unlike the British government, these elections use proportional representation, where the number of seats are allocated based on the number of votes that each party receives.

The Opposition

In the House of Commons, the second largest party (currently Labour) is named the opposition. This party is naturally in opposition to the government in power, and normally becomes the ruling party if they win the General Election. Just as the ruling party are led by the Prime Minister, the opposition also have a leader. At present, this is Jeremy Corbyn. This leader appoints what is known as a 'shadow cabinet', who challenge the current government and put forward different ideas and alternatives to current policies which they don't agree with.

Civil Service

The Civil Service is run by civil servants. These people assist the government in implementing its policies, and in delivering public services. They are appointed by an application process, and then answer to ministers, who act as their superiors. Civil servants are expected to remain politically neutral, and operate via a specific code of conduct/values, demonstrating integrity, honesty and objectivity at all times.

Wales, Scotland and Northern Ireland

In the last two decades, Wales, Scotland and Northern Ireland have been given far more control over matters which have an impact on their country. Both Wales and Scotland have had their own parliaments since 1999. This was also the case for Northern Ireland, but theirs has been suspended on a number of occasions since its introduction. The UK government retains the power to suspend these parliamentary bodies, and has done so in Northern Ireland on several occasions.

Scottish Parliament

Scotland was given its own parliament in 1999, and the Scottish Parliament is located in Edinburgh – the capital of Scotland. There are currently 129 Scottish Parliament members, who can pass laws for Scotland on matters such as:

- Health
- Education
- Tax issues
- Criminal law

Members of the Scottish Parliament meet in Holyrood, which is open to visits from the public. To arrange a visit or tour, you should contact the Scottish Parliament directly.

Welsh Parliament

Wales has its own government, called the National Assembly for Wales. These are located in Cardiff – the capital city of Wales. There are 60 Assembly members, with elections being held every 4 years. Debates are held in either Welsh or English, and Assembly publications are made in both languages. The Assembly has the power to pass laws of Wales, on matters such as:

- Education
- Economic and social development
- Housing
- Health services

Members of the National Assembly meet in Senedd, Cardiff. This building is open for tours and visits from the public, but you'll need to contact the Assembly Booking Service directly in order to arrange this.

The Northern Ireland Assembly

The Northern Ireland Assembly has a long and troubled history. First established in 1922, it has become a victim of Irish struggles, and was abolished in 1972 following The Troubles. In 1998, the Assembly was established again, after the Good Friday Agreement. There are 108 members of the Northern Ireland Assembly. Like the Welsh and Scottish governments, these are elected using a form of proportional representation. The Assembly has the power to make decisions on matters such as:

- Environmental issues
- Health services
- Education
- Social services

The Northern Ireland Assembly meets in Stormont, Belfast. Members of the public can visit Stormont by contacting the Education Service, or a member of the parliament directly.

Now test out what you've learned, with our revision quiz! You'll find full mock tests at the back of this book.

Revision Quiz

Q1. What is the Monarch's primary role in modern day Britain?

Q2. What is the name for the National Anthem of the United Kingdom (2016)?

Q3. What is democracy?

Q4. Why does Britain not have a written constitution?

Q5. Name three of the main political parties in the UK.

Q6. Where does the Prime Minister of the UK live?

Q7. There are two parliamentary houses in the UK, the House of Commons and the House of Lords. To which house does the Prime Minister belong to?

Q8. What is the role of a civil servant?

Answers

1. The primary role of the Monarch is to act as an ambassador for the UK, and strengthen international relations.

2. God Save The Queen.

3. Democracy is a system of a government where every member of the adult population is given the right to influence national decisions.

4. Britain has never had any revolution or uprising which required the government to create a constitution.

5. The Conservative Party, the Labour Party, the Green Party.

6. 10 Downing Street, London.

7. The House of Commons.

8. Civil Servants assist the government in implementing its policies, and delivering public services.

UK ELECTIONS AND VOTING

Every five years, a General Election is held. This gives people the chance to vote for new MPs. New MPs can also be elected in the event that the current MP of a constituency resigns/is unable to continue with the role, in which case a new election in the area takes place. This is known as a by-election. The system in which MPs are elected is known as 'first past the post'.

In order to contact the MP for your area, there are a number of channels you can use. Firstly, you can attend a local 'surgery', where you can meet your MP in person to talk about local issues which are concerning you. If you wish to contact them directly, your local library will hold their contact details, as will www.parliament.uk. Alternatively, you can find details of your local MP in the *Yellow Pages,* or you can contact them via letter or telephone at their constituency office or via their office at the House of Commons.

Towns and cities in the UK are governed via democratic councils. These are known as local authorities. The majority of larger towns or cities have a single authority governing them. The local authorities for your area are expected to provide services for the community, using government funds and tax generated income. In many towns/cities, there is a mayor, who acts as the leader of the council.

In order to stand for election as an MP, you must be aged 18. It is not a requirement to run for one of the major political parties, but it's very unlikely that you will win unless you have been nominated to do so. The major parties are always looking for ways to get the public involved in their debates and help with elections. On the other hand, there are also groups such as the CBI (Confederation of British Industry) who act as pressure groups on the government. They represent the views of a particular sector of British industry, such as business. There are other pressure groups for areas such as the environment – Greenpeace, and human rights – Liberty.

Political interest is extremely high in the UK, and parliamentary proceedings are often broadcast on television, as well as being published in an official report. This is known as *Hansard*. The UK operates with a free press, meaning that newspapers and media in the UK are free from government control. You will generally find that many newspapers sway towards one political party or viewpoint, and often run campaigns that are geared towards support for this.

UK Law states that television and radio coverage of political parties must be balanced, meaning that the public are given all sides of the argument before coming to an educated decision on which way to vote.

Who is allowed to vote?

The UK has a democratic voting system, which has been established since 1928. The present voting age stands at 18 years old, and all UK-born and adult British citizens have the right to submit their vote in public elections.

To be able to vote, you must have submitted your name to the electoral register. To register for this, you should contact your local electoral registration office. Alternatively, you can wait for the electoral register. This happens once every year, in September or October. During this period, a registration form is sent to every household in the UK and must be completed with the names of those in the household who are eligible and want to vote. You won't need to register to vote again unless you change address.

While this is applicable to England, Wales and Scotland, Northern Ireland uses a different system. Northern Ireland uses a system called individual registration, where those who wish to vote are required to fill in their own form.

In order to vote in any election, you will need to visit a polling station. Prior to election you will be provided with a poll card, which will inform you where your polling station is and the dates/times of the election. Polling stations are open from 7am until 10pm on the date of election. Different countries use different systems when you actually arrive at the station. In Northern Ireland, you'll have to bring photographic ID with you in order to vote. Once you have been given a ballot paper, you'll go into a private booth, fill in your vote and then put it into a ballot box. Nobody will know who you voted for, and the vote is entirely down to you. Instead of attending the polling station, you can also register for a postal ballot. In this instance, you'll be sent a ballot paper, which you'll then fill in at home and post back.

Who can run for office?

The majority of people in the UK, Irish Republic or the Commonwealth can run for public office. However, you must be aged 18 or over, and there are some exceptions to the rule. For example, members of the House of Lords cannot stand for election in the House of Commons.

You cannot run for public office if you are:

- A member of the armed forces.

- A civil servant.

- Someone who has certain previous criminal offences.

Now test out what you've learned, with our revision quiz! You'll find full mock tests at the back of this book.

Revision Quiz

Q1. How many years pass between General Elections in the UK?

Q2. What is the name for the system in which MPs are elected?

Q3. How old do you need to be to run for an election?

Q4. What is *Hansard*?

Q5. In the UK, the media and newspaper run independently, free from government control. True or false?

Q6. What is the electoral register?

Q7. What is a polling station?

Q8. Not everyone in the UK can run for public office. Give two examples of people who cannot run for public office.

See the next page for the answers!

Answers

1. 5 years.

2. First past the post.

3. 18 years old or older.

4. *Hansard* is the official written report on Parliamentary proceedings.

5. True.

6. The electoral register is a register of every person in the UK who has signed up/registered to vote. You must be on the electoral register in order to vote.

7. A polling station is a place where voters go to submit their votes for elections.

8. Civil servants, members of the armed forces.

UK LAW AND ORDER

In order to live in the UK, it's essential that you can understand and adhere to UK laws. Understanding why certain laws exist, and how you can ensure that you are following them, is one of the first steps to becoming a fully integrated British citizen. If you don't respect the law, then you can't expect to function as a member of society.

In this section, we'll give you a detailed breakdown of the legal system in Britain, and the laws that you'll need to follow. Britain is proud of being a welcoming country, but all residents, regardless of their background, are expected to comply with the law and to understand that some things which may be allowed in other legal systems are not acceptable in the UK. You should make sure that you are aware of the laws which will impact your everyday life, including both your personal and business affairs.

UK Law

Every person in Britain is subject to the same laws and treatment. The law applies in the same way to every single person. In Britain, there are two types of law:

- **Criminal Law.**

Criminal law applies to crimes which are investigated by the police or another authority, and can be punished by courts. For example:

- o **Drugs**. Selling or possessing drugs, such as ecstasy, cocaine or heroin, is illegal.

- o **Racism**. In the UK, it is a criminal event to cause offence to someone based on their religion or ethnicity.

- o **Weapons**. It's illegal to carry weapons, such as guns or knives, on your person; even if it's just for self-defence.

- o **Smoking in public places**. It's against UK law to smoke in almost every single public place, and you'll see signs which tell you this.

- o **Selling tobacco.** It is illegal to sell tobacco products to anyone under the age of 18.

o **Drinking in public.** Some places have alcohol-free zones where you cannot drink in public. The police can also confiscate alcohol or move people on from public places. You can be fined and arrested for breaking this law.

This list does not include all crimes. There are many that apply in most countries, such as murder, theft and assault. You can find out more about types of crime in the UK at www.gov.uk.

- **Civil Law**.

Civil law settles disputes between individuals/groups. For example:

o **Housing**. Housing law settles disputes between landlords and tenants, over home issues such as eviction.

o **Employment**. Employment law covers disputes over wages, unfair dismissal and other issues in the workplace.

o **Debt**. It's common for people to be taken to court if they owe significant amounts of money to someone.

o **Consumer Rights**. An example of this could be a dispute about faulty good or services.

How are these laws enforced?

Just as in any country, the laws of Britain are enforced by the police service. The UK Police Service consists of a number of separate constabularies, usually one for each area, which are headed by chief constables. They are independent of the government. The police is a public service that helps and protects everyone, no matter what their background or where they live. Police officers must themselves obey the law. They must not misuse their authority, make a false statement, be rude or abusive, or commit racial discrimination. If police officers are corrupt or misuse their authority, they will be severely punished.

The role of the police is to:

- Prevent crime and safeguard the public.

- Create a positive feeling in the community.

- Reassure the public.

The role of a police officer is far more varied than simply catching criminals. They play a huge role in community wellbeing and often are involved in local schemes and initiatives, all with the aim of benefitting the public. The UK police is a public service, who must behave with integrity. They are unbiased and protect everyone, regardless of their background or history. Since 2012, England and Wales have had elected Police and Crime Commissioners. These individuals are directly responsible for the delivery of an efficient police force, and are in charge of appointing Chief Constables. They also set local police priorities and the local policing budget.

Police Officers are supported in their role by PCSOs (Police Community Support Officers). PCSOs support officers at crime scenes, work directly with the public and patrol the streets. If you are arrested by the police, you will be taken to a police station. The officers will clearly explain why you have been arrested, and you will be able to seek legal help – such as a lawyer.

If something does go wrong with this process, the police complaints system tries to put it right. Anyone can make a complaint about the police by going to a police station or writing to the Chief Constable of the police force involved. Complaints can also be made to an independent body: the Independent Police Complaints Commission in England and Wales, the Police Complaints Commissioner for Scotland, or the Police Ombudsman for Northern Ireland.

UK Courts

Once a person has been charged with a crime, it is up to the court to decide how they will be dealt with. Depending on the seriousness of the crime, the person may be put on trial. Their fate will then be in the hands of a judge – a professional who is responsible for interpreting the law, and ensuring that trials run in a smooth and fair fashion. The government are not able to interfere with the outcome of a trial. Judges also preside over disputes between organisations or members of the public.

In England, Wales and Northern Ireland, minor criminal cases are dealt with in a Magistrates' Court. Perpetrators of serious crimes are tried at a Crown

Court. In Scotland, minor criminal offences go to a Justice of the Peace Court, whereas serious crimes are dealt with in a Sheriff Court. However, the most serious of cases (like murder) are dealt with at a High Court, in front of a judge and jury.

A jury consists of 12-15 members of the public, randomly selected from the local electoral register. If you are summoned for jury duty, it is a legal requirement that you attend/participate. The only exemption to this is if there are good reasons for not attending, such as being seriously ill or being illegible – which occurs if you have certain criminal convictions. The role of the jury is to listen to the evidence presented, and then collectively decide whether a person is guilty or not guilty. Scotland also has a 'not proven' verdict. If the jury finds a defendant guilty, then the judge will decide on a suitable penalty. If the jury finds the defendant not guilty, or reaches a verdict of 'not proven', the defendant walks away free. In England, Wales and Northern Ireland a jury has 12 members, and in Scotland a jury has 15 members.

Youth Court

In England, Wales, Scotland and Northern Ireland; the type of court that you attend will generally depend on your age. With the exception of especially serious cases, persons who are aged 10-17 will normally be judged in a Youth Court. Here, their case will be heard by a district judge, or by up to 3 special magistrates. Members of the public are not allowed to attend Youth Courts, and the media/papers cannot publish the names of the young person accused; nor release any photographs of them.

Scotland uses a slightly different system to judge young people. This is known as the Children's Hearing System. In Northern Ireland, a system of youth conferencing is used to decide how each child offender should be dealt with.

County Court

County Courts deal with civil disputes. For example, unpaid debts, injury compensation and divorce. While civil disputes are generally settled in a County Court, more serious civil cases are dealt with by the High Court in England, Wales and Northern Ireland. Scotland deals with such issues via a Court in Session, which is held in Edinburgh.

Minor monetary disputes have their own system, and are settled via what is known as small claims. The purpose of this system is to save each party the time and money that they would need for an ordinary court case, without using a lawyer. In England and Wales, the small claims procedure is used for claims that amount to £5000 or less. In Scotland and Northern Ireland, it is used for claims of £3000 or less. The interested parties will attend a small hearing in front of a judge, normally in an ordinary room, to resolve the dispute. Small claims can also be issued online through Money Claims Online (www.moneyclaim.gov.uk).

You can get details about the small claims procedure from your local County Court or Sheriff Court. Details of your local court can be found as follows:

- England and Wales: at www.gov.uk

- Scotland: at www.scotcourts.gov.uk

- Northern Ireland: at www.courtsni.gov.uk

Solicitors

If you are embroiled in a legal dispute, or have been charged with a crime, you can hire a solicitor. A solicitor is a type of lawyer who will provide you with advice on legal issues. They represent their clients in court and take action on behalf of their client. It's very easy to hire a solicitor in the UK, as there are a huge number of solicitors' offices. Alternatively, you can find a solicitor via the yellow pages, or by contacting the Citizens Advice Bureau. Before you hire a solicitor, make sure that you read up on them to check what type of law they specialise in, and whether they have the right amount of experience for you. Solicitors are generally quite expensive, so it's important to make sure that you are getting good value for your money.

Now test out what you've learned, with our revision quiz! You'll find full mock tests at the back of this book.

Revision Quiz

Q1. Give two examples of offences which can be charged under criminal law.

Q2. Give two examples of disputes which can be settled under civil law.

Q3. Who is in charge of appointing chief constables in England and Wales?

Q4. What is the role of a PCSO?

Q5. If you are summoned for jury duty, it is a legal requirement that you attend. True or false?

Q6. Scottish courts can deliver a verdict of 'not proven'. In this instance, what happens to the defendant?

Q7. What is the name for the system used to deal with monetary disputes of £5000 or less?

Q8. Members of the public can attend Youth Courts. True or false?

See the next page for the answers!

Answers

1. Carrying weapons, smoking in public places.

2. Housing disputes, employment disputes.

3. Police and Crime Commissioners.

4. PCSOs work to support police officers at crime scenes, patrol the streets and work directly with the public.

5. True, if you are summoned for jury duty you are legally obligated to attend.

6. They are released.

7. Small claims court.

8. False.

TYPES OF CRIME IN THE UK

The UK has a fairly low crime rate compared to the rest of the world, however it does face a number of threats. The biggest threat to the United Kingdom, at present, is from the so-called Islamic State and other like-minded organisations. Along with this, crimes such as paedophilia, fraud and drugs are high priority for British police chiefs.

Home-grown terrorism in the UK is statistically extremely low, and Britain has tight and effective border controls (to prevent terrorists from entering the country). However, anyone looking to make their home in the UK should be aware that it is a high priority for terrorist groups – as it is a rich, western country. To combat terrorist groups, the UK has established some of the most effective systems/organisations in the world, with intelligence services such as MI5 and GCHQ working every day to repel the threat.

The values established by the British people and government state that all people should be able to feel safe while living here, and should be protected from extremism. If you do feel that someone you know is part of an extremist group, or trying to persuade you to join too, you should immediately notify the police.

Your Rights as a British Citizen

As a British citizen, or even just as a resident of the UK, you fall under the freedom granted by the British government. Britain is one of the most liberal countries in the world, and has a high level of respect for individual rights. Britain played an essential role in the creation of the European Convention on Human Rights, which includes key details such as:

- The right to life.

- The right to a fair trial.

- The right to freedom of speech.

- The right to liberty.

Under UK law, it is a legal condition that all people are treated fairly; regardless of their age, sex, race, religion or beliefs etc. Discrimination is illegal.

Domestic Violence

Domestic violence in the UK is treated extremely seriously. Regardless of whether you are a man or a woman, violence towards your partner is a crime that can be prosecuted. If you have experienced domestic violence, then you should seek help as soon as possible, by contacting the Citizens Advice Bureau or a solicitor. There are also refuges in the UK, which are designed to shelter sufferers of domestic abuse, as well as emergency contact numbers in the *Yellow Pages.* Rape is illegal in the UK, and is regarded as an extremely serious offence. Any man who forces a woman to have sex, including a woman's husband, can be charged with rape.

Female genital mutilation (FGM), also known as cutting or female circumcision, is illegal in the UK. Practising FGM or taking a girl or woman abroad for FGM is a criminal offence.

Freedom of marriage in the UK is also an important aspect of society. Arranged marriage is perfectly acceptable – provided both parties agree. Forcing another person to marry you is a criminal offence, and the UK initiated measures to enforce this in 2007, with the Forced Marriage Act. Court orders can be obtained to protect a person from being forced into a marriage, or to protect a person in a forced marriage. Similar Protection Orders were introduced in Scotland in 2011. A potential victim, or someone acting on their behalf, can apply for an order. Anyone found to have breached an order can be jailed for up to two years for contempt of court.

In 2013, the Same Sex Marriage Act was introduced; making it legal for people of the same sex to be married.

Driving Laws

UK law states that you must be at least 17 years old to drive a car or motorbike, and 16 years old to drive a moped. In order to drive on public roads, you must first obtain a driving licence. To do this, you'll need to pass a driving test, which involves demonstrating both your knowledge and practical skills. You can use your license until you are 70 years old, after which time you'll need to re-test every 3 years. In Northern Ireland, newly qualified drivers must display an 'R' plate (for restricted driver) for one year after passing the test.

If your licence has been obtained from another country in the EU, you will be allowed to use this in the UK provided it's valid. This license lasts for 12 months, after which time you will need to obtain a UK driving licence. Please note that while this applies in 2016, we cannot guarantee that foreign driving licences will remain in place after Britain leaves the EU.

Furthermore, if you are a resident of the UK, you must register your vehicle with the Driver and Vehicle Licensing Agency. You'll be required to pay an annual vehicle tax, as well as paying for motor insurance. It's a criminal offence to drive without insurance. Finally, once your car is over 3 years old, you'll be legally required to get it tested by the Ministry of Transport (MOT) every single year. It is an offence not to have an MOT certificate if your vehicle is more than three years old. You can find out more about vehicle tax and MOT requirements from www.gov.uk.

Tax Evasion

Tax evasion in the UK is a serious offence, and is punished extremely seriously. In the UK, you are required to pay tax on your income. You'll need to pay tax on:

- Employment wages
- Self-employment profits
- Pensions
- Money generated by property and savings
- Taxable benefits

The money from your taxes goes towards essential services, such as roads or education. Generally, your income tax will be taken automatically out of your wages and paid directly to HM Revenue and Customs, the government department that collects taxes. This is known as Pay As You Earn (PAYE). Along with being taxed for paid work, you'll also need to pay National Insurance Contributions. These are automatically deducted from your wages by your employer, and used to pay for systems such as the National Health Service (NHS). Failing to pay enough National Insurance Contribution will result in you being unable to receive benefits such as a full retirement pension, or being unable to claim Jobseeker's Allowance.

If you are self-employed, then you will be required to pay your own taxes, and pay your own National Insurance Contribution. The former involves completing a tax return form, in a system called 'self-assessment'. If you need help with completing your taxes, you can find advice on the HRMC website. Alternatively, you could contact a tax advisor. If HRMC does send you a tax return, then it is important for you to complete and return the form as soon as you have all of the necessary information.

National Insurance Number

In order to pay your National Insurance Contribution, you will be given a National Insurance Number. This is a unique personal code, which ensures that your contributions are recorded against your name. In the UK, all young people are provided with a National Insurance number just before their 16th birthday. If you are a non-UK national looking for work, or setting up as self-employed, you'll need a National Insurance Number. Assuming that you have permission to work in the country, you'll need to telephone the Department for Work and Pensions. They will then arrange to provide you with a National Insurance number. You'll need to complete the application process, and attend an interview, before you can obtain this.

Being A Good Citizen

Once you have become a British citizen, there are certain responsibilities which you can fulfil, in order to become a great member of the community. While these are not obligatory, participating in the community is a great way to build relationships and make the most of your new citizenship. Now, let's look at some ways that YOU can become a great citizen.

British Values

As we have explained, Britain operates under a set of shared values and responsibilities, which ensure that public order is maintained and everyone gets along with each other. This is extremely important, and includes:

- Obeying the law.
- Respecting the rights of other citizens.
- Behaving in an ethical and responsible manner.
- Respecting the privacy of your neighbours.
- Keeping your garden clean and tidy.
- Recycling your rubbish, and taking your bins in after they've been emptied.
- Treating everyone equally.
- Helping your family.
- Voting in elections.

The better you exhibit these qualities, the easier it will become for you to integrate into society and become an active British citizen.

Supporting the Community

Part of being a good citizen involves working for the greater good of the community. There are a number of ways in which you can support the community:

- **Giving Blood.**

Giving blood is a great way to help the wider population. Donated blood is used by hospitals, to help people with injuries. In order to give blood, you must first register at www.blood.co.uk (England and North Wales), www.welsh-blood.org.uk (rest of Wales), www.scotblood.co.uk (Scotland) or www.nibts.org (Northern Ireland). Furthermore, you can also register as an organ donor at www.organdonation.nhs.uk. This means that when you die, it will be easier for your family to decide whether to donate your organs to those who need them. Alternatively, you can donate a kidney whilst still alive.

- **School Boards.**

By joining your child's school board, you can make a real difference to children's education. Members of the school board play an essential role in raising school standards, and are responsible for tasks such as:

    o   Improving overall school performance.

    o   Making sure the school are held accountable for their actions.

The best way to join the school board is to contact your local school directly. Alternatively, you can apply online at www.sgoss.org.uk.

- **Jury Duty.**

In the UK, any person on the electoral register can be selected at random to take part in jury duty. Jury duty means that you will serve on a jury during a court case. You must be aged 18-70 to take part in this, and it is a legal requirement (if selected) to attend.

- **Volunteering.**

Many people in the UK take part in voluntary work. There are many different types of voluntary work, but almost all of them involve helping the local community. For example, you could volunteer to work at a homeless shelter, or even to help with Alcoholics Anonymous meetings. You could mentor in a prison, help out at a residential care home or work with animals at a rescue centre. Alternatively, you could join the National Citizen Service programme, which provides 16-17 year olds with the chance to develop their skills and take part in community schemes.

- **Charity.**

Getting involved with charity is a great way to make a difference. There are thousands of charity organisations in the UK, who work to improve the lives of people and animals alike, as well as to protect the environment. These charities include:

o   The British Red Cross.

o   The National Society of the Prevention of Cruelty to Children.

o   Cancer Research UK.

o   The National Trust.

o   Friends of the Earth.

- **Recycling.**

Recycling is really important, and therefore people of the UK are encouraged to recycle wherever they can. Recycled materials are used to make new products, which means we take less materials from the earth, and reduce the amount of rubbish. As a British citizen, you are responsible for taking care of the area in which you live. While you won't be legally penalised for failing to recycle, you might find that your bin men (the people who take away the rubbish) eventually refuse to take your bins away, in an attempt to force you to recycle. Walking and using public transport are also good ways of recycling, as this creates less pollution than using a car.

Now test out what you've learned, with our revision quiz! You'll find full mock tests at the back of this book.

Revision Quiz

Q1. Domestic violence in the UK is treated as a minor offence. True or false?

Q2. In 2013, which legal act was passed, allowing the marriage of same sex partners?

Q3. How old do you need to be to drive a car or motorbike in the UK?

Q4. Name two forms of income which you'll need to pay tax on.

Q5. What does the money from taxes go towards?

Q6. What is a National Insurance Number?

Q7. What is the National Citizen Service programme?

Q8. Name two ways of reducing emissions/recycling.

See the next page for the answers!

Answers

1. False. Domestic violence in the UK is a serious crime.

2. The Same Sex Marriage Act.

3. 17.

4. Employment wages, Pension money.

5. The money from taxes goes towards essential services, such as roads and education.

6. If you are self-employed, then you will be required to pay your own taxes, and pay your own National Insurance Contribution. In order to pay your National Insurance Contribution, you will be given a National Insurance Number. This is a unique personal code, which ensures that your contributions are recorded against your name.

7. The National Citizen Service programme provides 16-17 year olds with the chance to develop their skills and take part in community schemes.

8. Walking and using public transport.

LIFE IN THE UK: MOCK TESTS

Hopefully by this point you'll have learned everything that you need to know, in order to secure your British citizenship. Now, it's time to test yourself.

Throughout this guide we've provided you with handy little revision tests, at the end of every chapter, to help you recap.

In this section, we'll give you 3 full mock Life in the UK Tests.

Take them one at a time and then compare your answers with those at the back the book. Please note, for the purpose of these mock tests, you will need additional paper. That way you can attempt these mock tests multiple times.

Just as in the real thing, each test should take no longer than 45 minutes to complete, and you'll need to achieve 75% to pass.

Good luck!

MOCK TEST 1

Q1. Which of the following is an overseas British territory?

A – The Falklands Islands

B – Wales

C – Hawaii

D – Northern Ireland

Q2. What were the supporters of James II known as?

A – The Cavaliers

B – The Roundheads

C – The Jacobites

D – The Suffragettes

Q3. Which two of the following were Irish missionaries?

A – St Augustine

B – St Columba

C – St Patrick

D – St Paul

Q4. Snowdon is the highest point of which country?

A – Wales

B – Northern Ireland

C – England

D – Scotland

Q5. People commemorate the 11th November by:

A – Wearing daffodils and attending church services

B – Wearing poppies and having a two minute silence

C – Praying and chanting the names of the dead

D – Giving each other gifts and presents

Q6. Prior to 'The Glorious Revolution', William of Orange was ruler of which country?

A – Germany

B – France

C – Scotland

D – The Netherlands

Q7. Which of the below statements is true?

A – In 1066, Harold Godwinson defeated William the Conqueror at the Battle of Hastings. Harold became King in December of the same year

B – In 1066, William the Conqueror defeated Harold Godwinson at the Battle of Hastings. William became King in December of the same year

Q8. Which of the following two people developed Penicillin into a useable drug?

A – Geoffrey Chaucer

B – Ernst Chain

C – Howard Florey

D – Roger Walpole

Q9. The Proms lasts 8 weeks, and celebrates which of the following:

A – Football

B – Rock music

C – Poetry

D – Orchestral music

Q10. Wimbledon is the only grand slam tennis tournament to be played on which surface?

A – Clay

B – Grass

C – Hard court

D – Sand

Q11. Today, Gaelic is still spoken in which country?

A – Wales

B – England

C – Northern Ireland

D – Scotland

Q12. What is the nickname for the huge bell outside of the Houses of Parliament?

A – Big Bong

B – Big Bill

C – Big Ben

D – Big Bell

Q13. Which of the following statements is correct?

A – Charles Dickens was the author of *Pride and Prejudice*

B – JK Rowling was the author of *Harry Potter and the Philosopher's Stone*

C – Jane Austen was the author of *Pride and Prejudice* and *Oliver Twist*

Q14. The Grand National is a:

A – Annual parliamentary meeting

B – Novel by Charles Dickens

C – Horse race

D – Football stadium

Q15. London Fashion Week takes place three times a year.

A – True

B – False

Q16. Which of the following statements is correct?

A – In the UK, Christmas is celebrated on the 25th December

B – In the UK, New Year's Day is celebrated on the 2nd of January

C – In the UK, Saint George's Day is celebrated on the 17th July

D – In the UK, Halloween is celebrated on the 13th April

Q17. The penalty for watching TV without a license can be up to:

A – A fine of £1000

B – 20 years in prison

C – Community service

D – Exile to Siberia

Q18. In which country will you find the cities of Birmingham and Plymouth?

A – Scotland

B – Wales

C – England

D – Republic of Ireland

Q19. In England, the minimum age required to play the National Lottery is:

A – 18 years old

B – 14 years old

C – 21 years old

D – 16 years old

Q20. In England, the name of any person who is charged with a crime can be released by the press.

A – True

B – False

Q21. In order to start work in the UK, you will need which of the following:

A – A state pension number

B – A birth certificate

C – A copy of *Harry Potter and the Philosopher's Stone*

D – A national insurance number

Q22. Who is the National Citizen Service Programme aimed at?

A – 14-15 year olds

B – 15-16 year olds

C – 16-17 year olds

D – 17-18 year olds

Q23. The laws, rules and regulations of Britain, are written down in an extensive document, which is known as The British Constitution.

A – True

B – False

Q24. The Act of Union 1707, united England with which of the following countries?

A – Scotland

B – Wales

C – Northern Ireland

D – The Republic of Ireland

MOCK TEST 2

Q1. In 1314, Robert Bruce led the Scottish army at which battle?

A – The Battle of Agincourt

B – The Battle of Culloden

C – The Battle of the Somme

D – The Battle of Bannockburn

Q2. Becoming a resident of the UK means that you must:

A – Surrender your own values and beliefs

B – Agree to work within Britain

C – Agree to respect the values of the United Kingdom

D – Surrender your human rights and privileges

Q3. Which of the following statements is incorrect:

A – Northern Ireland is a part of Britain

B – The Republic of Ireland is part of Britain

Q4. Where are the Houses of Parliament located?

A – Westminster

B – Manchester

C – Holyrood

D – The River Thames

Q5. As a British citizen, you are responsible for taking care of the area in which you live.

A – True

B – False

Q6. Which of the following is not a right that is offered to citizens of the United Kingdom?

A – The right to a fair trial

B – The right to be free from discrimination

C – The right to free speech

D – The right to watch television free of charge

Q7. Following their citizenship ceremony, new citizens of the UK will need to write a letter to the Queen, pledging the oath of allegiance.

A – True

B – False

Q8. Which of the following statements is correct?

A – Being a British citizen grants you the right to free speech, and this includes hate speech, discrimination and criticism of the government

B – Being a British citizen grants you the right to free speech. While this does not include hate speech, you have the right to voice criticism of the government

C – Being a British citizen grants you the right to free speech, but this does not include hate speech, discrimination or criticism of the government

Q9. One of the following countries is not part of Great Britain. Which is it?

A – England

B – Wales

C – Scotland

D – Northern Ireland

Q10. Which of the following does the term UK stand for?

A – The United Kingdom of Great Britain, Scotland and Northern Ireland

B – The United Kingdom of Great Britain and Northern Ireland

C – The United Kingdom of Great Britain, Wales, Scotland and Northern Ireland

D – The United Kingdom of Great Britain

Q11. What is the Domesday Book?

A – A diary that William the Conqueror kept of all his victories

B – Britain's oldest surviving public record

Q12. The population of the UK is spread evenly across England, Scotland, Wales and Northern Ireland.

A – True

B – False

Q13. The leader of the Gunpowder Plot was:

A – Guy Fawkes

B – Robert Catesby

C – Winston Churchill

D – Katie Noakes

Q14. The Monarch of the UK has the power to select the Archbishop of Canterbury.

A – True

B – False

Q15. The BAFTAs are the British equivalent of:

A – The IPG awards

B – The Balon d'Or

C – The Nobel Prize

D – The Oscars

Q16. Charlie Chaplin was an actor in which type of films:

A – Action movies

B – Silent movies

C – Romantic comedies

D – Political drama

Q17. Which of the following statements is correct:

A – April Fool's Day is celebrated on the 1st April. People play practical jokes on each other all day

B – April Fool's Day is celebrated on the 2nd April. People play practical jokes on each other all day

C – April Fool's Day is celebrated on the 1st April. People play practical jokes on each other until midday

Q18. What is the name for British currency?

A – British Pound

B – Sterling Pound

C – Frank

D – Bitcoin

Q19. Where in the UK would you go in order to exchange currency?

A – The supermarket

B – The embassy

C – The leisure centre

D – The post office

Q20. What type of church is the national Church of Scotland?

A – Catholic

B – Protestant

C – Mormon

D – Presbyterian

Q21. If you feel that somebody is trying to persuade you to commit acts of terror, or considering doing so themselves, what should you do?

A – Keep it to yourself

B – Inform the police

C – Quietly discuss it with them

D – Call an ambulance

Q22. The House of Lords is more influential than the House of Commons.

A – True

B – False

Q23. In 2016, the people of Britain voted to remain in the EU.

A – True

B – False

Q24. Which type of court usually deals with divorce cases?

A – Family court

B – Magistrate's court

C – County court

D – High court

MOCK TEST 3

Q1. In the UK, there are various laws in place to ensure that people at work are not treated differently because of their race.

A – True

B – False

Q2. Where do members of the Northern Ireland Assembly meet?

A – Westminster

B – Belfast

C – Dublin

D – Galway

Q3. Who is the head of state in the UK?

A – The Prime Minister

B – The Archbishop of Canterbury

C – The Monarch

D – The Pope

Q4. In order to vote in parliamentary elections, you will need to have your name on the electoral register.

A – True

B – False

Q5. You can use an EU driving licence in the UK for a period of:

A – 18 months

B – 6 months

C – 12 months

D – 4 weeks

Q6. Drivers in the UK must register their vehicle with:

A – Ofcom

B – Ofsted

C – The Motoring Registration Commission

D – The Driver and Vehicle Licensing Agency

Q7. Which of the following people is in charge of each individual police constabulary?

A – Chief Constable

B – PCSO

C – Chief Lieutenant

D – Crime Commissioner

Q8. In the UK, it is a criminal offence to carry a weapon for self-defence.

A – True

B – False

Q9. During the Battle of Waterloo, Britain was led by Admiral Nelson

A – True

B – False

Q10. In which year was the voting age changed, from 21 to 18?

A – 1950

B – 1951

C – 1969

D – 1962

Q11. The Chartists campaigned for which of the following?

A – Every region should have an equal say in elections

B – Every person over the age of 70 should have a bigger say in elections

C – People under the age of 14 should be able to vote

D – People who were unemployed should be able to run for election

Q12. Queen Elizabeth I re-established which church as the official Church of England?

A – Catholic

B – Protestant

Q13. Membership of the Commonwealth is voluntary.

A – True

B – False

Q14. In the year 1776, 12 colonies in North America declared independence from the British Empire.

A – True

B – False

Q15. The rapid development of industry during the 18th and 19th centuries in Britain, was named:

A – The Industrial Revolution

B – The Glorious Revolution

C – The Industrial Recognition

D – The Glorious Imposition

Q16. During the American War of Independence, Britain was allied with Spain and France.

A – True

B – False

Q17. Why was George I so reliant on his ministers?

A – He spoke very poor English

B – He was in poor health

C – He was medically catatonic

D – He was not intelligent

Q18. Failing to pay National Insurance will mean that you are ineligible to receive which two of the following benefits:

A – Jobseekers Allowance

B – Full retirement pension

C – Ability to run for prime minister

D – A reduction on driving insurance

Q19. Every person living in the UK has the right to choose their own religion.

A – True

B – False

Q20. Which of the following is a Jewish festival, commemorating the Jews' struggle for freedom?

A – Hannukah

B – Diwali

C – Christmas

D – Eid al-Fitr

Q21. Where will you find West End Theatres?

A – Cardiff

B – Edinburgh

C – Miami

D – London

Q22. Valentine's Day is celebrated on which day?

A – 12th July

B – 16th February

C – 19th April

D – 14th February

Q23. The Magna Carta established that:

A – The King was completely above the law and could do whatever he wanted

B – The King was subject to laws

C – Parliament had more power than the King

D – Parliament did not need to consult with the King before raising taxes

Q24. Mary Stuart was also known as:

A – Mary Queen of Scots

B – Bloody Mary

ANSWERS TO MOCK TESTS

Mock Test 1

Q1. Which of the following is an overseas British territory?

Answer: A – The Falklands Islands (p14)

Q2. What were the supporters of James II known as?

Answer: C – The Jacobites (p46)

Q3. Which two of the following were Irish missionaries?

Answer: B and C – St Columba, St Patrick (p24)

Q4. Snowdon is the highest point of which country?

Answer: A – Wales (p140)

Q5. People commemorate the 11th November by:

Answer: B – Wearing poppies and having a two minute silence (p101)

Q6. Prior to 'The Glorious Revolution', William of Orange was ruler of which country?

Answer: D – The Netherlands (p46)

Q7. Which of the below statements is true?

Answer: B – In 1066, William the Conqueror defeated Harold Godwinson at the Battle of Hastings. William became King in December of the same year. (p25)

Q8. Which of the following two people developed Penicillin into a useable drug?

Answer: B and C – Ernst Chain, Howard Florey (p78)

Q9. The Proms lasts 8 weeks, and celebrates which of the following:

Answer: D – Orchestral music (p104)

Q10. Wimbledon is the only grand slam tennis tournament to be played on which surface?

Answer: B – Grass (p124)

Q11. Today, Gaelic is still spoken in which country?

Answer: D – Scotland (p91)

Q12. What is the nickname for the huge bell outside of the Houses of Parliament?

Answer: C – Big Ben (p132)

Q13. Which of the following statements is correct?

Answer: B – JK Rowling was the author of Harry Potter and the Philosopher's Stone (p114)

Q14. The Grand National is a:

Answer: C – Horse Race (p124)

Q15. London Fashion Week takes place three times a year:

Answer: B – False (P118)

Q16. *Which of the following statements is correct?*

Answer: A – In the UK, Christmas is celebrated on the 25th December (p97)

Q17. *The penalty for watching TV without a license can be up to:*

Answer: A – A fine of £1000 (p109)

Q18. *In which country will you find the cities of Birmingham and Plymouth?*

Answer: C – England (p94)

Q19. *In England, the minimum age required to play the National Lottery is:*

Answer: D – 16 years old (p129)

Q20. *In England, the name of any person who is charged with a crime can be released by the press.*

Answer: B – False (p172)

Q21. *In order to start work in the UK, you will need which of the following:*

Answer: D – A national insurance number (p179)

Q22. *Who is the National Citizen Service Programme aimed at?*

Answer: C – 16-17 year olds. (p181)

Q23. *The laws, rules and regulations of Britain, are written down in an extensive document, which is known as The British Constitution.*

Answer: B – False (p154)

Q24. *The Act of Union 1707, united England with which of the following countries?*

Answer: A – Scotland (p48)

Mock Test 2

Q1. In 1314, Robert Bruce led the Scottish army at which battle?

Answer: D – The Battle of Bannockburn (p28)

Q2. Becoming a resident of the UK means that you must:

Answer: C – Agree to respect the values of the United Kingdom (p16)

Q3. Which of the following statements is incorrect:

Answer: B – The Republic of Ireland is part of Britain (p14)

Q4. Where are the Houses of Parliament located?

Answer: A – Westminster (p158)

Q5. As a British citizen, you are responsible for taking care of the area in which you live.

Answer: A – True (p182)

Q6. Which of the following is not a right that is offered to citizens of the United Kingdom?

Answer: D – The right to watch television free of charge (p109)

Q7. Following their citizenship ceremony, new citizens of the UK will need to write a letter to the Queen, pledging the oath of allegiance.

Answer: B – False (p17)

Q8. Which of the following statements is correct?

Answer: B – Being a British citizen grants you the right to free speech. While this does not include hate speech, you have the right to voice criticism of the government. (p17)

Q9. One of the following countries is not part of Great Britain. Which is it?

Answer: D – Northern Ireland (p14)

Q10. Which of the following does the term UK stand for?

Answer: B – The United Kingdom of Great Britain and Northern Ireland (p14)

Q11. The Chartists campaigned for which of the following?

Answer: A – Every region should have an equal say in elections (p25)

Q12. The population of the UK is spread evenly across England, Scotland, Wales and Northern Ireland.

Answer: B – False (p90)

Q13. The leader of the Gunpowder Plot was:

Answer: B – Robert Catesby (p101)

Q14. The Monarch of the UK has the power to select the Archbishop of Canterbury.

Answer: A – True (p97)

Q15. The BAFTAs are the British equivalent of:

Answer: D – The Oscars (p107)

Q16. Charlie Chaplin was an actor in which type of films:

Answer: B – Silent movies (p106)

Q17. Which of the following statements is correct:

Answer: C – April Fool's Day is celebrated on the 1st April. People play practical jokes on each other until midday. (p100)

Q18. What is the name for British currency?

Answer: A – British Pound (p91)

Q19. Where in the UK would you go in order to exchange currency?

Answer: D – The Post Office (p91)

Q20. What type of Church is the national Church of Scotland?

Answer: D – Presbyterian (p97)

Q21. If you feel that somebody is trying to persuade you to commit acts of terror, or considering doing so themselves, what should you do?

Answer: B – Inform the police (p176)

Q22. The House of Lords is more influential than the House of Commons.

Answer: B – False (p156)

Q23. In 2016, the people of Britain voted to remain in the EU.

Answer: B – False (p15)

Q24. Which type of court usually deals with divorce cases?

Answer: C – County court (p172)

Mock Test 3

Q1. In the UK, there are various laws in place to ensure that people at work are not treated differently because of their race.

Answer: A – True (p176)

Q2. Where do members of the Northern Ireland Assembly meet?

Answer: B – Belfast (p161)

Q3. Who is the head of state in the UK?

Answer: C – The Monarch (p151)

Q4. In order to vote in parliamentary elections, you will need to have your name on the electoral register.

Answer: A – True (p165)

Q5. You can use an EU driving license in the UK for a period of:

Answer: C – 12 months (p178)

Q6. Drivers in the UK must register their vehicle with:

Answer: D – The Driver and Vehicle Licensing Agency (p178)

Q7. Which of the following people is in charge of each individual police constabulary?

Answer: A – Chief Constable (p170)

Q8. In the UK, it is a criminal offence to carry a weapon for self-defence.

Answer: A – True (p169)

Q9. During the Battle of Waterloo, Britain was led by Admiral Nelson.

Answer: B – False (p54)

Q10. In which year was the voting age changed, from 21 to 18?

Answer: C – 1969 (p154)

Q11. The Chartists campaigned for which of the following?

Answer: A – Every region should have an equal say in elections (p154)

Q12. Queen Elizabeth I re-established which church as the official Church of England?

Answer: B – Protestant (p37)

Q13. Membership of the Commonwealth is voluntary

Answer: A – True (p14)

Q14. In the year 1776, 12 colonies in North America declared independence from the British Empire.

Answer: B – False (p55)

Q15. The rapid development of industry during the 18th and 19th centuries in Britain, was named:

Answer: A – The Industrial Revolution (p53)

Q16. During the American War of Independence, Britain was allied with Spain and France.

Answer: B – False (p55)

Q17. Why was George I so reliant on his ministers?

Answer: A – He spoke very poor English (p51)

Q18. Failing to pay National Insurance will mean that you are ineligible to receive which two of the following benefits:

Answer: A and B – Jobseekers Allowance, Full retirement pension (p179)

Q19. Every person living in the UK has the right to choose their own religion.

Answer: A – True (p176)

Q20. Which of the following is a Jewish festival, commemorating the Jews' struggle for freedom?

Answer: A – Hannukah (p98)

Q21. Where will you find West End Theatres?

Answer: D – London (p112)

Q22. Valentine's Day is celebrated on which day?

Answer: D – 14th February (p100)

Q23. The Magna Carta established that:

Answer: B – The King was subject to laws (p29)

Q24. Mary Stuart was also known as:

Answer: A – Mary Queen of Scots (p39)

GLOSSARY

AD Anno Domini. Referring to the number of years after the birth of Jesus Christ – used as a time reference.

Allegiance. Loyalty to something – for example, to a leader, a faith or a country.

Annexed. Joined.

Architect. Someone who designs buildings.

Armed Forces. The army, navy and air force which defend a country in times of peace and war.

Arrested (police). Taken by the police to a police station and made to stay there to answer questions about illegal actions or activity.

Arson. The criminal act of deliberately setting fire to something.

Assault. The criminal act of using physical force against someone or of attacking someone – for example, hitting someone.

Bank holiday. A day when most people have an official day off work and many businesses are closed. A bank holiday can also be called a public holiday.

Baron. A man who has one of the ranks of the British nobility. The title was particularly common during the Middle Ages.

BC Before Christ. Referring to the number of years before Jesus Christ was born – used as a time reference.

Bishop. A senior member of the clergy in the Christian religion, often in charge of the churches in a particular area.

Boom. A sharp rise in something – very often in business activity or the economy.

Brutality. Behaviour towards another which is cruel and violent and causes harm.

By-election. An election held in a parliamentary constituency or local authority area to fill a vacancy (see also General Election).

Cabinet (government). A group of senior ministers who are responsible for controlling government policy.

Casualties (medical). People who are wounded or killed (for example, in a war).

Cathedral. The most important church in an area.

Charter (government). An official written statement which describes the rights and responsibilities of a state and its citizens.

Chieftain. The leader of a clan in Scotland or Ireland.

Civil disobedience. The refusal of members of the public to obey laws, often because they want to protest against political issues.

Civil law. The legal system that deals with disputes between people or groups of people.

Civil service. The departments within the government which manage the business of running the country – people who work for the government can be called civil servants.

Civil war. A war between groups who live in the same country.

Clan. A group of people or families who live under the rule of a chieftain and may be descendants of the same person – a term used traditionally in Scotland.

Clergy. Religious leaders, used here to describe religious leaders in Christian churches.

Coalition. A partnership between different political parties.

Colonise. Inhabit and take control of another country. People who colonise are called colonists.

Commemorate. Show that something or someone is remembered.

Composer. Someone who writes music.

Conquered. Beaten in battle.

Constituency. A specific area where the voters who live in that place can elect an MP to represent them in Parliament.

Constitution (legal). The legal structure of established laws and principles which is used to govern a country.

Convention (government). An agreement, often between countries, about particular rules or codes of behaviour.

Criminal law. The legal system that deals with illegal activities.

Decree (legal). Official order, law or decision.

Democratic country. A country which is governed by people who are elected by the population to represent them in Parliament.

Devolution. The passing of power from a central government to another group at a regional or local level, which can then be called a devolved administration.

Dialect. A form of language spoken by a particular group or people living in a particular area.

Domestic policies. Political decisions that relate to what is happening within a country (as opposed to in another country).

Electoral register. The official list of all the people in a country who are allowed to vote in an election.

Electorate. All the people who are allowed to vote in an election.

Eligible. Allowed by law.

Ethnic origin. The country of birth, someone's race or the nationality of someone when they were born/the customs and place from which a person and their family origination (or came from).

Executed. Killed as a punishment.

First past the post. A system of election in which the candidate with the largest number of votes in a particular constituency wins a seat in Parliament.

Franchise. The right to vote.

General Election. An event in which all the citizens of a country who are allowed to vote choose the people they wish to represent them in their government.

Gothic. A type of art or architecture that is based on the Middle Ages.

Government policies. Official ideas and beliefs that are agreed by a political party about how to govern the country.

Guilty. Found by a court to have done something which is illegal.

Heir. Someone who will legally receive a person's money or possessions after their death. The heir to the throne is the person who will become the next king or queen.

House (history). A family (e.g. House of York).

House of Commons. The part of the Houses of Parliament where MPs who are elected by the voting public debate political issues.

House of Lords. The part of the Houses of Parliament where people who have inherited their place or been chosen by the government debate political issues.

Household. A home and the people who live in it/something that relates to a home. For example, household chores are tasks that are done around the house, such as cooking and cleaning.

Houses of Parliament. The building in London where the House of Commons and the Houses of Lords meet.

Illegal. Something which the law does not allow.

Infrastructure. Structured network that is necessary for successful operation of a business or transport system – for example, roads or railways.

Innocent (legal). Found by a court not to have done something illegal.

Judge. The most important official in court. The judge makes sure what happens in court is fair and legal.

Judiciary. All the judges in a country. Together, they are responsible for using the law of the land in the correct way.

Jury (legal). People who are chosen to sit in court, listen to information about a crime, and decide if someone is guilty or innocent.

Legal. Allowed to do so by law.

Legislative power. The power to make laws.

Liberty. Freedom.

Magistrate. A person who acts as a judge in a court case, where the crime is not a serious one.

Marital status. Information about whether a person is single, married, separated or divorced. This is often asked for on official form.

Media, the. All the organisations which give information to the public, i.e. newspapers, magazines, television, radio and the Internet.

Medieval/Middle Age. In history, the period between 1066 and about 1500.

Missionary. Someone who travels to teach about a religion.

Monarch. The king or queen of a country.

National issues. Political problems that can affect everyone who lives in a country.

Nationalised. Bought and then controlled by central government – relating to an industry or service that was previously owned privately.

Nobility. The people in a country who belong to the highest social class, some of whom may have titles – for example, Lord, Duke, Baron.

Office, to be in. To be in power in government.

Olympics. International sporting event held every four years.

Opposition. In the House of Commons, the largest political party which is not part of the government is officially known as the opposition.

Oratorio. A single piece of music for an orchestra (musicians) and singers, often about a religious idea.

Pale (history). Part of Ireland governed by the English.

Party politics. The shared ideas and beliefs of an organised group of politics.

Patron saint. A Christian saint who is believed to protect a particular area or group of people.

Penalty (legal). Punishment for breaking the law.

Plague. A very serious, infectious disease.

Pope, the. The head of the Roman Catholic Church.

Portrait. A picture of a person.

Practise a religion. Live according to the rules and beliefs of a religion.

Presbyterian. The main Protestant Church in Scotland.

Prime Minister. The politician who leads the government.

Prohibit/prohibition. Make something illegal.

Proportional representation. A system of election in which the political parties are allowed a number of seats in Parliament, that represents their share of the total number of votes cast.

Protestants. Christians who are not members of the Roman Catholic Church.

Public body. A governmental department or a group of people who represent or work for the government, and who work for the good of the general public.

Public house/pub. A place where adults can buy and drink alcohol.

Quakers. A Protestant religious group.

Rebellion. Organised fighting against a government.

Reformation, the. The religious movement in the 16th century that challenged the authority of the Pope and established Protestant churches in Europe.

Refugee. A person who must leave the country where they live, often because of a war or for political reasons.

Residence. The place where someone lives.

Rival viewpoints. Opinions held by different groups of people.

Rural. Countryside.

Scrutinise. Examine all the details.

Seat (parliament). A constituency.

Sentence. A punishment imposed by a court.

Shadow cabinet. Senior MPS of a political party not in government.

Sheriff (legal). A judge in Scotland.

Slavery. A system in which people bought and sold other people (slaves) who were forced to work without pay.

Sonnet. A poem which is 14 lines long and rhymes in a particular way.

Speaker, the. The member of the House of Commons who controls the way issues are debated in Parliament.

Stand for office. Apply to be elected – for example, as an MP or councillor.

Strike, to go on. Refuse to work in order to protest against something.

Successor (government). A person who comes after another and takes over an office or receives some kind of power – for example, a son who becomes king when his father dies is his successor.

Suspend. To stop something from happening or operating, usually for a short time.

Terrorism. Violence used by people who want to force a government to do something. The violence is usually random and unexpected, so that no one can feel really safe from it.

The Phone Book. A book which contains names, addresses and phone numbers of organisations, business and individuals.

Theft. The criminal act of stealing something from a person, building or place.

Trade union. An association of workers formed to protect its members.

Treaty. An official written agreement between countries or governments.

Uprising. A violent revolt or rebellion against an authority.

Voluntary work. Work which someone does because they want to and which they do for free, i.e. they do not receive any payment.

Volunteer. Someone who works for free or who offers to do something without payment (see voluntary work).

War Effort. The work people did in order to help the country in any way they could during wartime.

Yellow Pages. A book that lists names, addresses and telephone numbers of businesses, services and organisations in an area. Also available online at www.yell.com.

Life in the UK Test

100s more practice questions for free!

www.MyLifeInTheUKTest.net

NEED A LITTLE EXTRA HELP WITH BECOMING A BRITISH CITIZEN?

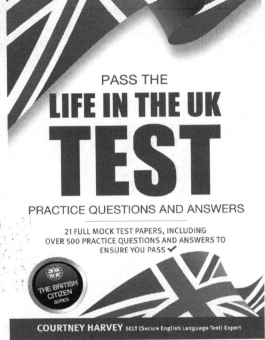

How2become have created two other FANTASTIC guides to help you prepare for the British citizenship tests.

These exciting guides are filled with essential tips and tricks, to ensure that your preparation is thorough, and that you are completely ready for the process ahead. With our help, you can secure your British citizenship today!

FOR MORE INFORMATION ON OUR GUIDES, PLEASE CHECK OUT THE FOLLOWING:

WWW.HOW2BECOME.COM